REVERE FRANKLIN WEIDNER

Anthropology

The Doctrine of Man

First published by Just and Sinner 2019

Copyright © 2019 by Revere Franklin Weidner

Copyright 2019 Just and Sinner. All rights reserved. The original text is in public domain, but regarding this updated edition, besides brief quotations, none of this book shall be reproduced without permission.

Permission inquiries may be sent to JustandSinner@yahoo.com

Just and Sinner. http://www.jspublishing.org

Third edition

ISBN: 978-0-9967482-1-6

This book was professionally typeset on Reedsy. Find out more at reedsy.com

Contents

PREFACE.	v
Introduction	viii
ANTHROPOLOGY OR THE DOCTRINE OF MAN.	viii
The Creation and Constitution of Man	1
§ 1. The Creation of Man.	1
§ 2. The Essential Constituents of Man.	12
§ 3. The Unity of the Race.	22
§ 4. The Propagation of the Soul.	27
The Original Condition of Man	34
§ 1. The Scripture Teaching.	34
The Idea of Man.	35
§ 2. The Church Doctrine.	45
The Fall	55
The Divisions.	55
§ 1. The Biblical Account.	55
§ 2. The Historical Actuality of the Fall.	57
§ 3. The Dogmatic Statement of the Doctrine.	60
§ 4. Attempts to Explain Away Historical Facts.	62
Original Sin	65
The Divisions.	65
§ 1. The Scripture Doctrine.	66
§ 2. The Church Doctrine.	67
The Essential Character of Sin	118
Divisions.	118
§ 1. The Doctrine of Scripture.	118
§ 2. The Church Doctrine.	127

Moral Bondage, or the Doctrine of Free Will	154
Divisions.	154
§ 1. The Scripture Doctrine.	155
§ 2. The Church Doctrine.	157
Select Literature	190
Examination Questions	193
EXAMINATION QUESTIONS ON ANTHROPOLOGY.	193

PREFACE.

This book is the outgrowth of thirty years of discussion in the class room. Five great works lie at the foundation of this presentation of the Scriptural teaching of the Doctrine of Man as understood and taught by those who believe in God's inspired Word, and especially as confessed by that large and rapidly increasing Church, known as the first Protestants in history.

The first work is Luthardt's *Kompendium der Dogmatik* from which this book contains a faithful translation (with many additions), of all that portion bearing on Man, Sin, and Free-Will, covering some thirty pages in the original. Of the merits of Luthardt's summary we need not speak. Its numerous references to the literature of the subject have often led the writer into the study of the deeper things of man's nature and of God's revelation.

A second work is Krauth's Conservative Reformation, one of the greatest classics in Theology, noted not only for its contents but also for its English style, and which contains the ablest treatise on Original Sin to be found in the English language, a synopsis of which is given at its proper place in this book.

The third work is Delitzsch's System of Biblical Psychology, first studied by the writer forty years ago, and its subject ever since a favorite field of investigation. Without question this is the greatest and most suggestive work ever written on the

Nature of Man. It was regarded as his greatest work by Dr. Delitzsch himself, to whom the author in many things owes more than may appear.

The fourth work is the great book of Julius Mueller on The Christian Doctrine of Sin, the deepest work on this subject ever written as well as the greatest. Though very speculative in some parts, yet in most points here at issue, its treatment of the subject is more closely allied to the theology of the Confessions of the sixteenth century than is the case in most of the recent systems, in that it asserts the reality of guilt and the necessity of objective atonement. The spirit in which Mueller entered upon his investigation can be seen by his own confession and the statement of the principle that would guide him. He says: "From the time when the author sat as a scholar at the feet of the beloved and revered NEANDER, the conviction has been deeply-rooted in his mind, that Christianity is a practical thing, that everything in it is connected more or less directly with the great facts of SIN and of REDEMPTION, and that the plan of Redemption, which is the essence of Christianity, cannot be rightly understood until the doctrine of SIN be adequately recognized and established . . . In our present inquiry, we must pause at every new stage of our investigation to ascertain our latitude, and to set ourselves right by the contents of Holy Scripture, and thus satisfy ourselves that we are not erring from the right way."

The fifth work is the System of Christian Ethics by Harless, which among all the great German works written from the Christian standpoint, takes the first place in depth, spiritual insight and scriptural illustrations. This is the same Dr. Harless who has written on Ephesians; of whom Bishop Ellicott, that great commentator, has said: "I am deeply indebted to the admirable exposition of Harless on Ephesians, which, for accurate scholarship, learning, candor, and ability, may be pronounced one of the best, if not the very best commentary that has ever yet appeared on any single portion of Holy Scripture."

We have given the results of the investigations of these divines on the topics at issue, and if thereby we do nothing more than bring the reader in contact with these gifted minds and their spiritual insight, the undertaking has its ample reward.

An analytical table of contents, an index, and a series of questions with which the work ends will be found to be a means of great practical helpfulness in the study of the subject therein presented.

The author is greatly indebted to the Rev. Alfred Ramsey, D. D., Ohio Professor of Ecclesiastical History in Chicago Lutheran Theological Seminary, Maywood, IL, for the reading and criticism of his manuscript, and for the care with which he has read the final proof.

And now I send these pages forth with the earnest prayer that they may be blessed to the furtherance of the cause of truth and righteousness, and that they may be the means of opening to many the rich treasures of God's Word.

R. F. W

Easter, 1912.

CHICAGO LUTHERAN THEOLOGICAL SEMINARY, MAYWOOD, IL.

Introduction

ANTHROPOLOGY OR THE DOCTRINE OF MAN.

INTRODUCTION

The system of Christian Doctrine may be treated under thirteen heads:

1. Introduction or Prolegomena;[1]
2. The Doctrine of God;[2]
3. The Doctrine of Man;
4. The Doctrine of the Person of Christ;
5. The Doctrine of the Work of Christ;
6. The Doctrine of the Work of the Holy Spirit;
7. The Doctrine concerning the Church;
8. The Doctrine of the Church;[3]
9. The Doctrine of Holy Scripture;
10. The Doctrine of Holy Baptism;

---

[1] See my Introduction to Dogmatic Theology. Second revised edition. Pages 287. Chicago, 1895

[2] See my Theologia, or The Doctrine of God. Pages 144. Chicago, 1902.

[3] See my Ecclesiologia, of The Doctrine of God. Pages 120. Chicago, 1903.

11. The Doctrine of the Lord's Supper;
12. The Doctrine of the Ministry;[4]
13. The Doctrine of the Last Things.

Under Anthropology the following seven topics will be discussed:

1. Man
   2. The Original Condition of Man
   3. The Fall
   4. Original Sin
   5. The Essential Character of Sin
   6. Actual Sins
   7. Moral Bondage, or the Doctrine of Free Will

The topic Man will be treated under four heads:

1. The Creation of Man
   2. The Essential Constituents of Man
   3. The Unity of the Human Race
   4. The Propagation of the Soul

---

[4] See my Doctrine of Ministry. Pages 148. Chicago, 1907

1

The Creation and Constitution of Man

§ 1. The Creation of Man.

Hollaz: Man is an animal, consisting of a rational soul and an organic body, framed by God, and endowed at the first creation with God's own image, in order that he might 1) sincerely worship the creator, 2) live a godly life, and 3) attain eternal happiness.

In general, we may learn from the first two chapters of Genesis,

1) That man appears as the last work of the sixth day, raised above all the other animals whose creation preceded his, by being distinguished as related to God in a way altogether unique, for he was made "in the image, after the likeness" of God.

2) In Gen. 1:26, 27 we have a statement of the creation of man, in the abstract; in Gen. 2:7-25 a concrete and detailed description of the mode of the creation of the first man; not

different events, but different views.

3) From Gen. 1:26, 27 we learn that man is the result of specially deliberate and direct creative will.

4) From Gen. 2:7 we learn that man was formed from the existing "dust of the ground"; that the Creator "breathed into his nostrils the breath of life"; and thus "man became a living soul".

Gen. 1:26. And God said, Let us make man in our image, after our likeness.

Gen. 2:7. And Jehovah God formed man of the dust of the ground, and breathed into his nostrils the breath of life, and man became a living soul.

On the mode of this production Quenstedt expresses himself as follows:

It consists in this, that God made man

1) with singular deliberation taken concerning this work, Gen. 1:26

2) immediately, with his own hands, so to say

3) ornately and elegantly

4) successively (Gen. 2:7, 21, 22), first (with respect to Adam) forming the body, and then breathing into it a soul

We believe that Delitzsch expresses great truths when he amplifies the teaching of Gen. 2:7, as here summarized:

This one verse is of such deep significance that interpretation can never exhaust it. It is the foundation of all true anthropology and psychology. We must not represent to ourselves the process of creation in so anthropomorphic a manner as is usually employed. Scripture gives us no justification in assuming that God formed a clod of earth with His hands into a human form, and standing near it, breathed into it, from without, the breath of life. Man came into existence, as did also the other creatures, as a work of divine omnipotence operating invisibly, and only appreciable in its results.

Herein is distinguished the creation of man, in that while all other creatures were called into being by means of a distribution of existing materials, by the divine command of power going forth to the earth, no such mighty command goes forth in the case of man, but a solemn word of self-determination precedes and the creation of man is an act of Gods immediate formation. In respect to his internal nature, man's origination is absolute and whole, not by means of the distribution of the entire impersonal natural life already existing, but by a direct act of God's breathing. Man, thus, was created otherwise than were the living beings inferior to him.

From Gen. 2:7, we learn that the body of man came into existence prior to the soul.

1) Scripture everywhere assumes that man is a nature originating first of all in respect to his earthly corporeality, composite, and on that account a limited and mortal nature. The coming into being of man is an ascending, gradual progression. It begins with the earthly basis of his existence, in order that man may never forget that he is a mortal who has the earth as his ancestor (Ps. 10:18, "man who is of the earth").

2) That the body of man, in order to unite all elements into itself, is formed from earth, the most composite of the elementary forms, -indeed out of dust, therefore of the finest portions of the earthly material. The body of the first-created man was the highest of all concentrations of the possibilities of glorification contained in Eden.

3) That the body of man was formed by God, not merely externally and mechanically, like a massive statue, formed man-like in its outline but in its inward parts unarticulated. The

general prior conditions of life were present, but they were not yet combined into a living unity. When God breathed into the material body the breath of life, this material was penetrated with Power, articulated, and organically combined, and then man became an organic individuality, an organism living of itself, "a living soul".

4) God breathes forth from himself into the bodily form and endows the human body with the relative spirit which henceforth is to belong to man's own nature. In other words; the human spirit came into being by a free and immediate personal operation of God. When this spirit of life is associated with the body, man becomes a living soul. The soul does not live by itself. The spirit in man is the source of man's soul, and the ultimate source is the Spirit of God. Man was endowed with soul by means of God's inbreathing the breath of life. That man received a self-subsisting spirit, is, in truth, the fundamental assumption of the Holy Scripture. Paul expressly distinguishes the sell-conscious spirit of man from the self-conscious Spirit of God (1 Cor. 2:11). Spirit and soul are never separated and may be apprehended as only two distinct sides of one principle of life. The soul is the bearer and the mediator of the life that proceeds from the spirit of man. The spirit is superior to the soul. The soul is the product, or more expressively, the manifestation of the spirit.

5) The inbreathing into the nostrils can only be meant to affirm that God, by means of his breath, brought forth and united with the bodily form the same principle of life which became the source of all the life of man, and announced its existence thenceforth by the breath passing into and out of the

nostrils.⁵

Man, like all beings endowed with life originated from two elements, 1) from earthly material, (ground, dust), and 2) from the Divine Spirit (*ruach*), Gen. 2:7, compared with Ps. 104:29, 30; 146:4. As in general the soul (*nephesh*) originates in the flesh (*basar*) by the union of spirit with matter, so in particular the human soul arises in the human body by the breathing of the divine breath into the material frame of the human body.⁶

Oehler especially elaborates the thought that man did not originate from the beast. The soul, which is common to man and beast, does not originate in both in the same way. The souls of animals arise, like plants from the earth, as a consequence of the divine word of power; Gen. 1:24, "let the earth bring forth the living *nephesh*". Thus the creating Spirit which entered in the beginning (Gen. 1:2) into matter, rules in them; their connection with the divine spring of life is through the medium of the common terrestrial creation. But the human soul does not spring from the earth; it is created by a special act of divine breathing (Gen. 2:7 compared with Gen. 1:26). The human body was formed from the earth before the soul; in it, therefore, those powers operate which are inherent in matter apart from the soul (a proposition which is of great importance, as Delitzsch rightly remarks).

But the human body is still not an animated body; the powers existing in the material frame are not yet comprehended into a unity of life; the breath of life is communicated to this frame directly from God, and so the living man originates.

Thus the substance of the human soul is the divine spirit

---

[5] See DELITZSCH, System of Biblical Psychology, pp. 87-102.

[6] See OEHLER, Theology of Old Testament. Page 70.

of life uniting itself with matter. The earthly materials do not become flesh until the *ruach* or spirit has become united therewith (Gen. 6:17, "flesh, wherein is the breath of life;" 7:15; Job 12:10; 34:14, 15). As the soul sprang from the spirit, and contains the substance of the *ruach* or spirit as the basis of its existence, the soul exists and lives also only by the power of the *ruach*. In order to live, the soul which is called into existence must remain in connection with the source of its life. When in Job (33:4) we read:

"The spirit of God hath made me,

And the breath of the Almighty giveth me life"—the first sentence expresses the way in which the human soul is called into being; the second, the continuing condition of its subsistence.

In the soul, which sprang from the spirit, and exists continually through it, lies the individuality,—in the case of man his personality, his self, his ego; because man is not *ruach*, spirit, but has it—he is soul.

We have purposely quoted so fully, and with approval, the presentations of Delitzsch and Oehler, because in these days of the general acceptance of speculative and evolutionary hypotheses, it is refreshing to read the clear teaching of two of the greatest Old Testament scholars that ever lived, in opposition to the false theories emerging from the fertile minds of negative Old Testament critics and modern scientists.

Pantheism

In general the pantheistic theory of the universe is at all points in deadly antagonism to the teaching of the Bible.

It negatives all the cardinal Christian ideas—the personality of God, the creation of the world, the freedom of man, the reality of sin, providence, redemption, and immortality. The radical principle of the theory is that God and the world are one. It denies to God any being distinct from the world, and to the world any being distinct from God.

It conceives of God either as spirit or as substance; in the first case there results an idealistic form of pantheism, in the latter a materialistic. To all practical intents the two are common. Wherever the pantheistic theory is accepted, polytheism prevails.

In particular pantheistic anthropology is at all points antagonistic to Christian thought.

1. In all its forms it degrades man.

Our mind is neither more nor less than the idea of our body. Mind and body are the same thing conceived of under different aspects, under the attribute of thought as mind, under the attribute of extension as body. When the body is dissolved, the mind perishes along with it.

2. It denies true personality.

Neither God nor man possesses personality. The individual man is a mere temporary manifestation and individualization of the great impersonal spirit of nature.

3. It denies human freedom.

Human actions of whatever nature are subject to the inexorable law of causality, and moral distinctions are purely relative.

4. It denies moral responsibility.

There is no purpose in events. All things proceed by an eternal necessity of nature, and with the greatest possible perfection, but without design or final causes. This doctrine implies that even moral evil, as we call it belongs to the eternal order, and is in reality good.

5. It denies individual immortality.

It mocks at the idea of a life that survives death, and declares that with the last breath individual existence ends. The finite spirit then loses itself in the infinite, like a bubble in a stream.[7]

The Evolutionary View

The favorite hypothesis of our day regarding the origin of man is in general, that man derives his present civilization, by long and slow progression, from savage human ancestors; that these, again, were developed during an indefinite series of ages out of some form or family of the animal tribes; and this hypothesis grows out of a theory of evolution, applicable to all animated life, that in the course of ages too vast to be conceived, all living things evolved from the simplest cellular forms of life.

Many investigators, basing their theories on the study of embryology, paleontology, and experiments in breeding animals and plants, have come to the conclusion that man is the result of a process of development or evolution, some

---

[7] See the able discussion on The Pantheistic Theory in BRUCE, Apologetics, pp. 71-90.

primeval ape being his immediate ancestor. This view has been advanced by Darwin, Huxley, Lubbock, Tylor, Haeckel, Schmidt, and others.

With reference to this view Zoeckler, a well-known apologist and theologian, says: In general, we may say that a large body of competent scientific inquirers object to the whole theory of gradual transformism, as well as its application to the human race.

Among the objections are:

1) The purely hypothetical character of the theory of Evolution forbids its being received as Science;

2) There are scientific objections to the theory from the absence of necessary links;

3) The enormous lapse of time demanded for the origination of species by insensible modifications is too great.

With reference to the first objection that it is only a hypothesis Zoeckler develops the statement:

1) There are anatomical differences between man and even the most developed apes, so important that the assumption of their common origin is subject to the greatest difficulties.

2) No validity can be attached to the embryological proof, as Haeckel asserts. Other authorities on the doctrine of evolution decidedly disagree with Haeckel.

3) The proof from paleontology is also full of gaps and deficiencies.

4) Not one case of a definite and permanent change of an organic species into another has been accurately observed. As far as empirical knowledge goes, the character of the individual vegetable and animal species bas never changed.

5) Geology shows that the specific groups of organic beings were distinct from the very beginning.

6) The Darwinian hypothesis of descent does not give due consideration to the great difference in a psychological respect between man and animal.

Man is distinguished from all preceding organisms 1) by his freedom, 2) self-consciousness, and 3) endowment of speech. Conservative investigators like Agassiz, Rudolph Wagner, Wigand, and Dubois-Reymond have always ridiculed the hypothesis that considers the higher nature of man as the product of a purely natural development.[8]

Equivocal or Spontaneous generation, revived as an hypothesis by Haeckel and some other evolutionists, and called Abiogenesis by Huxley, indicates the view that living or organic matter can be produced from that which is not in itself living matter, in other words from inorganic matter. It is opposed to Biogenesis, the view that living matter can be produced only from that which is itself living. Both of these words were coined by Huxley in 1870.

We simply have to say,

1) No instance of the production of living forms from inorganic matter has ever been adduced. It is contrary to all known facts.

2) Nearly all modern writers on physiology maintain that there is no such thing as spontaneous generation.

3) The famous Dr. Virchow says: Of spontaneous generation we do not possess any actual proof, and who ever supposes it has occurred is contradicted by the naturalist, and not merely by the theologian.

---

[8] See ZOECKLER, article Man in New Schaff- Herzog; LAIDLAW, The Bible Doctrine of Man, pp. 284-297; DAWSON, Modern Ideas of Evolution; JOHNSON, The Christian's Relation to Evolution; PAULIN, No Struggle for Existence. No Natural Selection. 1908.

4) It has been well said: Spontaneous generation is a fiction in ethics, as it is in psychology and biology. The moral cannot be derived from the non-moral, any more than consciousness can be derived from the unconscious, or life from azoic rocks.

The eminent scientist and geologist Dawson makes the following statement concerning the antiquity of man:

"As a geologist, and as one who has been in the main of the school of Lyell, and after having observed with much care the deposits of the more modern periods on both sides of the Atlantic, I have from the first dissented from those of my scientific brethren who have unhesitatingly given their adhesion to the long periods claimed for human history, and have maintained that their hasty conclusions on this subject must bring geological reasoning into disrepute, and react injuriously on our noble science. We require to make great demands on time for the pre-human periods of the earth's history, but not more than sacred history is willing to allow for the modern or human age."

All the arguments from Geology in favor of a great antiquity for man have been carefully summarized by Dawson in his famous "Origin of the World," and after closely examining the nature and amount of the evidence, he sums up the discussion in the words of another eminent geologist: "In short, if we say that, hypothetically, the whole first known human age occurred within 4000 years of the Christian era, no one can say that it is geologically impossible."[9]

---

[9] See DAWSON, Origin of the World, pp. 263-321. 1893; DAWSON, Meeting Place of Geology and History.

§ 2. The Essential Constituents of Man.

We are not to regard man as simply consisting of body and soul, but of body, soul, and spirit.

Delitzsch[10] says: There are such various kinds of views of dichotomy and trichotomy that, in general, neither conformity with, nor opposition to, Scripture, can be predicated of either.

Scripture speaks at one time in a definitely dichotomic strain, as in Matt. 6:25, "be not anxious for your life (*psuche*) . . . nor yet for your body (*soma*);" and James 2:26, "the body (*soma*) apart from the spirit (*pneuma*) is dead;" at another, in a strain as absolutely and undeniably trichotomic, as in 1Thess. 5:23, "may your spirit and soul and body be preserved entire;" and Heb. 4:12, "piercing even to dividing of soul and spirit."

There is a false trichotomy, and in opposition thereto a scriptural dichotomy, and there is a false dichotomy, and in opposition to it a scriptural trichotomy.

No one has entered more deeply, or presented more clearly, this whole subject, than Delitzsch in his Biblical Psychology, and we largely condense and reproduce his statements.

Scripture requires us to regard man as the synthesis of two absolutely distinct elements, essentially opposed to each other, spirit and matter. Even on the first page of Scripture, matter and spirit are placed in essential opposition. And this opposition subsists not only between God's Spirit and chaos, but also between the spirit that endues man with soul, and the body of man. But with this decision in favor of the dualism of spirit and matter, the question of dichotomy or trichotomy is in nowise settled.

---

[10] See DELITZSCH, Biblical Psychology, pp. 103—119.

There were three errors which had to be combated in the early church, which made the orthodox teachers of the fourth and fifth centuries, and our older Lutheran dogmaticians, averse to the true biblical trichotomy which distinguishes between body, soul, and spirit.

These errors may be tersely stated as follows:

1) The pseudo-Gnostic view, that the spirit of man is a portion of Divinity incapable of sin, as Origen thought;

2) The Apollinarian error, that Christ had body and soul in common with us, but that the eternal Logos had in Him usurped the place of the human spirit, a narrowing of the true humanity of Christ;

3) The semi-Pelagian error, that the spirit of man is excepted from original sin, which according to their view affected only the body and soul.

The biblical view may be stated in these words:

1. Body, soul, and spirit are not three essentially distinct elements. The spirit and soul of man are to be distinguished as primary and secondary, but not with the view that the spirit and soul are substantially one and the same. Two passages, in this connection, claim special consideration, 1 Thess. 5:23 and Heb. 4:12.

1) In 1 Thess. 5:23 the apostle stringently analyzes the human constitution into spirit, soul, and body. But these three elements, to every one of which the work of sanctifying grace extends, are in nowise three essentially distinct elements.

2) So likewise in Heb. 4:12, there are two elements in the psychical life of man; how else could a dividing asunder of soul and spirit, which God's word effects in us, be spoken of?

The apostle's view, in the final result, is certainly dichotomic, body on the one hand, and soul and spirit, inseparably joined together, on the other.

2. But spirit and soul are of a similar nature. Spirit and soul are not two distinct natures, but two distinct elements in the psychical life of man. The body and the spirit of man are of distinct nature, but the soul belongs to the side of spirit.

Man has received his life-principle immediately from God. From this one principle are derived both his bodily his spiritual life. The body without the spirit is dead (James 2:26). There is no natural soul between spirit and body, but only a life of the soul that proceeds from the spirit itself. The spiritual or understanding soul and the bodily soul are in their essence and nature one. The one thing on which we must lay stress is that the soul is of one nature with the spirit.

3. The soul proceeds from the spirit. If, according to Scripture, the soul does not belong to the side of man's bodily nature, but to the side of his spirit it is either one and the same with his spirit, or else the soul proceeds from his spirit. The true view is that the soul, whether it be called substance or potentiality, is not the spirit itself, but another nature conditioned by the spirit, although standing incomparably nearer to it than to the body. Possibly it is best to say, the spirit and soul are of one nature, but of distinct substances.

Delitzsch and Zezschwitz agree in the definition of the spirit of man. The *pneuma* or spirit, is with perfect justice defined by Von Zezschwitz as the highest spiritual power, comprehending, ruling, penetrating all the powers of the soul and the body in the power of its own connection with God. The main proof is the important passage, Gen. 2:7, "Jehovah God . . . breathed into his nostrils the breath of life, and man became a living soul."

The spirit stands in immediate causal relation to God, and for this reason all the divine operations having redemption in view address themselves first of all to the *pneuma* or spirit, and only thence attain to the *psuche* or soul, and when God manifests Himself He appeals to the spirit of man, and first of all man's spirit is renewed (Ps. 15:10, "renew a right spirit within me;" Tit. 3:5, "according to his mercy he saved us, through the washing of regeneration and renewing of the Holy Ghost").

The soul is the mediating link of the spirit and the body, the peculiar form of the personality of man. The spirit is the inbreathing of the Godhead, and the soul is the outbreathing of the spirit. The spirit is the life-center provided for the body, and the soul is the raying forth of this center of life. The spirit is the inward being of the soul, and the soul is the external nature of the spirit.[11]

We will in this connection also summarize Oehler's presentation of the Old Testament view of the constituent parts of man. Man perceives and thinks by virtue of the spirit which animates him (Job 32:8; Prov. 20:27), but the perceiving and thinking subject itself is the soul. The impulse to act proceeds from the spirit (Ex. 35:21, "every one whom his spirit made willing," Prov. 16:32, "he that ruleth his spirit"), but the acting subject is not the spirit, but the soul; the soul is the subject which sins (Ezek. 18:4).

In many cases, indeed, soul and spirit stand indifferently, according as the matter is looked upon, or to use Hofmann's words, according as "the personality is named after the special individual life, or alter the living power which forms the condition of its special character."

With this compare in particular Isa. 26:9, "with my soul have

---

[11] See DELITZSCH, Biblical Psychology, pp. 103-119.

I desired thee; yea, with my spirit within me will I seek thee earnestly." The second sentence does not say the same as the first, but, as shown by the particle yea, it ascends higher. "Yea, with my spirit," with the whole strength of my inward life.

From all this it is clear that the Old Testament does not teach a trichotomy of the human being in the sense of body, soul, and spirit, as being originally three coordinate elements of man; rather is the whole man included in the flesh and soul, which sprang from the union of the spirit with the matter or body (Ps. 84:2).

The spirit forms, in part, the substance of the soul individualized in it, and in part, after the soul is established, the power and endowments which flow into it.[12]

Especially suggestive is Oehler's presentation of the Old Testament teaching concerning the heart and its relation to the soul. The soul of man has a double sphere of life:

1) It is *anima*, that on which rests the life belonging to the senses, the soul of the flesh in the more limited sense. As such it acts in the blood, and supplies life to the body through the blood; hence the proposition, "The life (soul) of the flesh is in the blood" (Lev. 17:11); in· deed it is said directly "the blood is the life (soul)," Deut. 12:23; Lev. 17:14.

2) It is not simply *anima*, the principle of life belonging to the senses, but at the same time animus—the subject of all acts of knowing, feeling, and willing, and especially the subject of those acts and states of man that refer to his communion with God, Deut. 4:29, "Thou shalt find Jehovah, when thou searchest after him with all thy heart and with all thy soul;" 6:5.

---

[12] OEHLER, Old Testament Theology, § 70.

3) In both of its relations, as *anima* and *animus*, the soul centers in the heart. As the central organ of the circulation of the blood ("the pitcher at the fountain," Eccles. 12:6), the heart forms the focus of the life of the body.

4) The heart is also the center of all spiritual functions. "Keep thy heart with all diligence; for out of it are the issues of life," Prov. 4:23.

5) The moral and religious condition of man also lies in the heart. We read of a wise heart (Prov. 10:8), of a clean heart (Ps. 51:10), of a perverse or forward heart (Ps. 101:4), of a stubborn and evil heart (Jer. 3:17), etc.

6) Hence all revelation addresses itself to the heart, even the revelation of the law, Deut. 6:6; for it demands love to God from the whole heart, and starting from this center, also from the whole soul (Deut. 11:18).

7) Faith, in which man's personal life in its deepest basis takes a new direction, belongs entirely to the sphere of the heart (Ps. 112:7; compare the same view in New Testament, Rom. 10:9, 10).

8) But frames of mind and emotions are just as often predicated of the soul as of the heart, and in Old Testament, grief and care, fear and terror, joy and confidence, tranquility and contentment, are referred sometimes to the heart (Dent. 28:65; Ps. 28:7) and sometimes to the soul (Ps. 6:4; 42:6).

Bernhard Weiss very fully discusses the New Testament teaching concerning the nature of man, and in substance says: The ideas are largely the same as in the Old Testament, even to the peculiar transformation which they have received in the Pauline System.

1. The body. The essential substance of the human body is flesh (*sarx*). The corporeity of man is formed of earthy matter.

The body mediates and brings about man's connection with nature. The flesh and body are subject to death (1 Pet. 3:18; John 6:51) and corruption (Acts 2:31).

2. The soul. The flesh of living man is flesh possessed of a soul, and the soul has its seat in the blood.

1) The soul is the bearer of the bodily life, which is prolonged by nourishment (Matt. 6:25); for so long as the soul is in man he lives (Acts 20:10). The soul requires the body for its own perfect life. The blood can be conceived of as the principle of the propagation of the bodily life of man (John 1:13; Heb. 2:14). If the blood is shed the soul departs (Matt. 23:35; Mark 14:24). The soul forms the central point of the life of the individual, and in it lies his personality. The soul of the flesh is the subject of all sensuous feelings (Luke 12:19), appetites (John 1:13) and lusts (1 Pet. 2:11; 2 Pet. 2:18).

2) As the soul owes its origin and endowment to the divine breath of life which was breathed into the earthly material (Gen. 2:7), it is also the bearer of the spiritual life in man.

3. The spirit. The spirit of man is independent of his corporeity. If the spirit quits the body, man is dead (Matt. 27:50); without the spirit, the body is dead (James 2:26).

The spirit, however, is not only the principle of the bodily life in man, but also of the higher spiritual life. The soul is only the bearer of both and the raying forth of this center of life. It is in the spirit that purposes are formed (Acts 19:21); in the spirit zeal dwells (Acts 18:25) as well as meekness (1 Pet. 3:4). The spirit is the subject of every higher feeling. As the bearer of Christian life it is endangered by the sensuous lusts (1 Pet. 2:11), subverted by heresy (Acts 15:24), and can be guarded (1 Pet. 2:25; 4:19) and purified (1 Pet. 1:22).

The spirit does not die at death (Matt. 10:28), but is only

separated from the body. Soul and spirit are inseparably united, and when souls are separated from the body (Rev. 6:9; 20:4), they are pure spiritual essences (1 Pet. 3:19; Heb. 12:23) and continue to exist as spirits (1 Pet. 4:6).

4. The heart. The central organ within man is the heart, which is conceived of as the seat of the whole spiritual life in man (1 Pet. 3:4; Heb. 13:9). It is in the heart that thoughts dwell (Matt. 9:4; Luke 2:35; 24:38). It is the seat of self-consciousness and of consciousness of truth (Heb. 10:22; 1 John 3:19-21). It is the seat of all feelings (Acts 2:26), of all inclinations (Matt. 22:37), of all lusts (Mark 7:21-23), and of all resolutions (Acts 5:3, 4).

The nature of man is known by that which proceeds from the heart, as the tree is known by its fruit (Matt. 7:15-20; 12:33-35).[13]

Materialism

Materialism is a most thoroughgoing opponent to Christian Anthropology. It is not a science but a system of philosophical speculation. It may be called the gospel of the flesh. It is the foe at present in the ascendant. The main cause lies in the progress of physical science within the present generation.

In general, as a summary of its teachings, we may say:

1) It denies the existence of a personal and independent soul, of immortality and all belief in another world. There is no spirit, no soul; the agency of matter is everything.

---

[13] WEISS, Biblical Theology of New Testament. Vol. 11 pp. 120—125; WEIDNER, Biblical Theology of New Testament. Vol. 1, pp. 77-81.

2) With characteristic boldness, some of its most Prominent advocates maintain that thought is a secretion of the brain like bile of the liver, and that all feelings and thought are modes of action. Consciousness is regarded as but an attribute of matter. All psychical phenomena are explained by physical states, thought by motion.

3) The materialist repudiates all belief in human freedom. Men are automata, not like brutes, unconscious but conscious, and having an idea that they are voluntary agents, but they are not. We do what we like, and we like what we must. For proof appeal is made to the results of the modern science of statistics. There are physical causes at work determining the actions of men with as much certainty as the occurrences of eclipses. Conduct is the necessary result of nature. Will results from a condition of the brain produced by external influence. The criminal is a man whose brain and nervous system are more or less diseased; the virtuous man is one whose whole body is in a normal state of health.

4) To speak of the ethical and religious aspects of a system which recognizes no God but atoms, may appear like mockery. It makes conscience an outgrowth of the social instinct. All religion is merged in the worship of the universe. The universe as a whole is conceived of as revealing to the instructed eye an aesthetic, a rational and a moral order; the first appealing to and satisfying the sense of beauty and harmony, the second supplying the intellect with materials for devout contemplation, the third embodying the idea of the good, and offering to the conscience a satisfactory substitute for a righteous God. Materialism, thus, would destroy all the moral

faculties.[14]

There are three facts that are utterly destructive of materialistic opinions.

1. The fact of mental consciousness. If all thought is but the brain's own product, what sets it thinking? The motive power must be of a mental nature. How can self-consciousness, the highest effect of the mental power, be designated a mere action of the brain, when it is rather that most purely mental act, the soul's knowledge of itself, by which man separates himself from all that is about him, and comprehends and thinks of himself in his oneness with himself? It is absurd to call that a product of matter, which is an abstraction from all matter.

2. The fact of moral consciousness. My conscience is as much a fact as my body. It is not a result of experience or of education, or of persuasion, but is an inward moral voice. It may be obscured or perverted yet it still exists in every human being.

3. The fact of religious consciousness. There is an inward attraction of man toward a higher power, reflected and attested by his consciousness. This feeling is common to all forms of faith, however dim it may be, and however obscured by superstition. The fact of its existence must be acknowledged, but its existence would be an impossibility if nothing exists but that which is the product of matter.

It is on these three facts that the whole higher life of man depends.[15]

---

[14] See BRUCE, Apologetics, pp. 90-115.

[15] See LUTHARDT, Fundamental Truths of Christianity, pp. 126-135.

§ 3. The Unity of the Race.

The Scriptural doctrine concerning man is that mankind is not only of the same species, but also derived from a common origin, descended from Adam. The most important passages bearing on this point are:

Gen. 1:27, 28—"And God created man in his own image, in the image of God created he him; male and female created he them. And God blessed them: and God said unto them, Be fruitful, and multiply, and replenish the earth, and subdue it;"

2:71—"And Jehovah God formed man of the dust of the ground, and breathed into his nostrils the breath of life; and man became a living soul;"

2:22,—"And the rib, ·which Jehovah God had taken from the man, made be a woman, and brought her unto the man;"

3:20,—"And the man called his wife's name Eve; because she was the mother of all living;"

Acts 17:26,—"And he made of one every nation of men to dwell on all the face of the earth."

It is also implied in Gen. 9:19; Rom. 5:12; 1 Cor. 11:8, 9; 1 Tim. 2:13.

Four considerations drawn from history and science corroborate the teaching of Scripture.

1. The argument from history.

The traditions of the races largely point to a common origin and ancestry in Central Asia. The history of the successive migrations of man explains the way in which mankind was distributed from one center. Modern ethnologists generally agree that the Indian races of America are related to the Mongolians of Asia, and came over either through Polynesia or by way of the Aleutian Islands.

SAYCE: "The evidence is now all tending to show that the districts in the neighborhood of the Baltic were those from which the Aryan languages first radiated, and where the race or races who spoke them originally dwelt."

2. The argument from philology.

The languages of mankind point to a common origin. The Indo-Germanic languages can be traced to a primitive tongue, of which Sanscrit is the oldest existing remnant. There is evidence that the old Egyptian language is a connecting link between the Indo-European and the Semitic tongues, that the Egyptians were immigrants from Central Asia, and that the Turanian, Semitic and Aryan branches had one common origin.

G. F. WRIGHT:[16] "Two or three thousand years of prehistoric time is all that would be required to produce the diversification of languages which appears at the dawn of history . . . The prehistoric stage of Europe ended less than a thousand years before the Christian era." The evidence of language is unanswerable.

3. The argument from psychology.[17]

The soul is the most important element in the constitution of every living creature. It is the same in kind in each distinct species. The souls of all men are essentially the same. They have in common the same animal appetites, instincts, and passions, and all share in those higher attributes which belong exclusively to man. They are endowed with reason, conscience and free will. They all stand in the same relation to God as spirits possessing a moral and religious nature, thus showing

---

[16] See WRIGHT, Man and the Glacial Period, pp. 242-301.

[17] See HODGE, Systematic Theology. Vol. 2, pp. 77-91.

they are of the same species and have a common origin.

4. The argument from natural science.[18]

We find nothing in the facts of natural science to render it doubtful that all mankind was derived from a single pair. Science establishes the fact that the whole human race is of one species. It of course cannot say whether the race has sprung from one Pair or not, but science demonstrates that the race might have sprung from one pair, inasmuch as they all belong to one species. What science shows to be possible, revelation distinctly teaches.

Science, moreover, enables us to make the following affirmations:

1. Science teaches us nature's law of parsimony. Nature is economical in its resources. There is no waste of means, and as one pair is sufficient to have originated the population of the globe, the scientific presumption is strong, that there was but one pair.

2) Only animals of the same species produce a permanently fertile offspring. But the children resulting from the union of the most widely diverse human races are permanently fertile.

3) It is the common judgment of comparative physiologists that man constitutes but a single species. The differences which exist between the various families of mankind are to be regarded as of varieties of this species.

4) Unity of species is presumptive evidence of unity of origin.

TYLOR: "On the whole it may be asserted that the doctrine

---

[18] See KRAUTH, Conservative Reformation and its Theology, pp. 366, 367.

of the unity of mankind now stands on a firmer basis than in previous ages."

Zoeckler advances the following evidence as favoring the theory of the unity of the human race.

1) The different races of men do not lose their power of procreation by intermarriage.

2) Among the human races, the skeleton, the period of pregnancy, and the average duration of life are the same

3) Apparent divergences of the races in the formation of the skull, the quality of skin, hair, etc., may be explained by climatic conditions.

4) Linguistic objections do not stand upon a solid basis

5) Archaeology and the science of religions furnish important material for the proof of the original unity of the human race.

6) The different races of humanity reveal a thoroughgoing uniformity and spiritual relationship in both a psychological and an ethical respect.[19]

Dr. Krauth lays especial stress on the importance of the doctrine of the unity of the human race. He emphasizes the fact that it is important in its bearing on the recognition of the equality and fraternity of all mankind. It is essentially connected with just views of original sin, and the true view of the nature of redemption. Although modern science has sometimes been perverted to the weakening of man's faith in this great doctrine, yet the most eminent men of science, whether Christian or not, have united in the judgment that science does not weaken, by any of its facts, the Scripture witness to the unity of the human race.

---

[19] See Article on Man in New Schaff-Herzog.

There are three principal hypotheses opposed to the Scripture doctrine.

1) The theory of the Coadamites, propounded by Agassiz, of different centers of creation. Agassiz assumes eight centers of creation for the human race, and held to eight corresponding types of humanity,—the Arctic, the Mongolian, the European, the American, the Negro, the Hottentot, the Malay, and the Australian. Though different in origin, he held them to be one in their intellectual and moral nature.

But the whole tendency of recent science has been adverse to the doctrine of separate centers of creation, even in the case of animal and vegetable life.

2) The theory of the Preadamites, that is, that there were men before Adam. This view was specially developed by Peyrerius in 1655 and recently revived by Winchell, who, however, does not deny the unity of the race, holding that Adam was not the first man, but simply the ancestor of the Jews. This view treats the Mosaic narrative as legendary rather than historical, and according to this theory Eve could not be "the mother of all living" (Gen. 3:20), nor could "through the one man's disobedience" "sin have entered into the world" (Rom. 5:12, 19).

3) The theory of Autochthons, that man originally sprang from the earth, either by spontaneous generation or evolution, the latter being the prevailing view with skeptical naturalists.

But science cannot present a shadow of trustworthy, direct evidence of the production of living forms from inorganic material.

§ 4. The Propagation of the Soul.

The origination of the human soul has been explained by three theories, known as Preexistence, Creationism and Traducianism.

1) Preexistence. This view was held by Plato, Philo, and Origen, but never met with general acceptance in the Church, and was expressly condemned at the Council of Constantinople in 553. Plato held that intuitive ideas, such as space, time, cause, substance, right, etc., are reminiscences of things learned in a former state of existence; Philo held that all souls are emanations from God; Origen explained the diverse conditions at birth by the differences in the conduct of these same souls in a previous state.

In modem times this theory has been advocated by Kant, Julius Mueller, Edward Beecher, and many modern poets, like Wordsworth and Tennyson. Kant attempts to explain radical evil in man by the decision made by him at some former time, and Julius Mueller, in his great work "On Sin," employs the theory to solve the problem of Original Sin.

In another form, the theory of Preexistence asserts simply that all souls were created at the beginning, by the word of God, and are united, at conception, with the material organism.

2) Immediate Creationism maintains that there is a creation of the soul by God, and that about the fortieth day after conception it is united with the embryo. The passages of Scripture to which appeal has been made to sustain this view are Jer. 38:16; Isa. 57:16; Zech. 12:1; Acts 17:25; Ps. 119:73; Job 10:12; 33:4; Num. 16:22; 27:16; and Heb. 12:9. Jerome asserts that this was the view of the Church, but this is an overstatement of the fact, although it was certainly the view of a number of the Fathers. It is the predominant view of the Roman Catholic Church, and most of the Reformed (Calvinistic) theologians maintain it, usually with the theory that by the union of the soul with the body the soul becomes sinful (after Luthardt and Krauth).

3) Traducianism, or mediate Creationism, is the theory that both body and soul are derived from the parents. The true theory of Traducianism is that the soul is a creation of God, of which the parents are the divinely ordained organ.

Of the theory of Preexistence it may be said:

1) It is opposed to the great fact of our human experience, as to the similarity between the soul of the parent and child.

2) It will not bear the test of logic, and only increases the difficulty of explaining the origin of sin. It simply throws back the question and does not answer it.

3) It is not only without the support of Scripture, but is directly contradicted by the general drift of Scripture, specially by Gen. 3, and by the whole argument in Romans 5:12.

Of the theory of Immediate Creationism it may be said:

1) The strongest of Scripture passages quoted to sustain it, implies no more than that the spirit of man has higher attributes than his body, is preeminent as the work of God, and the chief seat of his image, without at all implying that God's creation of the soul is a direct or immediate one. For instance, when in Isa. 57:16 we read of "the souls that I have made," it with equal clearness declares in Ps. 139:13, "thou didst form my reins" (kidneys, inward parts), and in Jer. 1:5, "I formed thee in the belly"—yet we do not hesitate to interpret these latter passages of mediate Creationism. The truth of Creationism is the presence and operation of God in all natural processes, and the recognition of individuality.

2) This view involves at its root unconscious Gnosticism. It makes matter capable of sin and of imparting sinfulness;

3) On this theory, no man could call his child really his own,—certainly he would not be the father of the child's highest part. It would mean that only the body is propagated.

4) There is no escaping the inference that it makes God the author of Sin. According to this theory, God creates a perfect, spotless, holy soul, and places it into a body which will inevitably pollute it.

This is the decisive argument against Creationism. The theory is utterly irreconcilable with the sinful condition of the human soul. And this has led many Reformed theologians to modify their Creationism by combining it with Traducianism.

Of Traducianism, or the theory of mediate Creationism, we may say:

1) This theory corresponds with the prevailing and clear statements of the Scriptures, as in Gen. 5:3; Acts 17:24-26.

2) It is the doctrine absolutely demanded by the existence of original sin, and by the doctrine that God is not the author of sin. Only Adam had the right to be a Creationist.

3) This view is defended among the Fathers, especially by Tertullian, Athanasius, Gregory of Nyssa, and many others. Augustine remained undecided, confessing his ignorance, yet leaning strongly to Traducianism, and implicitly holding the view. The Lutheran Divines with few exceptions are Traducian. The expressions in the Symbolical Books, such as in the Catechism, "I believe that God has created me," and in the Formula of Concord, "God has created our souls and bodies after the fall," are meant of the mediate Creationism, not of the direct or immediate.

4) This theory agrees with the latest results of scientific inves-

tigations. Physical characteristics, as well as mental gifts,[20] and especially uniformly moral tendencies and dispositions,[21] are transmitted from parents to children, and this proves that we derive the soul, as well as the body, from our parents. Heredity is God's visiting of sin to the third and fourth generation. Dr. Holmes: "A man is an omnibus, in which all his ancestors are seated".

Quenstedt[22] very clearly presents the Scriptural proof.

1. The soul of the first man was immediately created by God;

2. But the soul of Eve was produced by propagation;

3. And the souls of the rest of men are created, not daily, nor begotten of their parents as the body or souls of brutes, but, by virtue of the divine blessing, are propagated, per traducem, by their parents. We prove this:

1) From the primeval blessing of God, Gen. 1:28, "And God blessed them, and God said unto them, Be fruitful, and multiply, and replenish the earth;" see 8:17, 9:1.

2) From God's rest and cessation on the seventh day from all work, Gen. 2:2;

3) From the production of the soul of Eve, Gen. 2:21, 22;

4) From the description al generation, Gen. 5:3, "And Adam begat a son in his own likeness, after his own image;"

5) From Gen. 46:26, "all the souls that came out of, the loins of Jacob;"

6) From the following absurdities, (a) if it be affirmed that

---

[20] See GALTON, Hereditary Genius.

[21] "That which is born of the flesh is flesh" (John 3:6).

[22] See SCHMID, Doctrinal Theology of the Evangelical Lutheran Church. Translated by Hay and Jacobs. Third edition, revised 1899. A work constantly referred to, and which must be in the possession of every Lutheran pastor.

souls are created immediately by God, either original sin would be altogether denied, or God could not be vindicated from injustice, and (6) it would follow that man does not beget an entire man, but only a part of one;

7) From Ps. 51:5 (7), "Behold, I was shapen in iniquity; and in sin did my mother conceive me."

Delitzsch gives a brief history and a complete defense of Traducianism in his famous work on Biblical Psychology, of which we here give a brief summary.

The importance of this topic in respect to the doctrines of the incarnation and of original sin is manifest. The ancient Latin Church abandoned the creationism of heathendom. In its fold, Tertullian was the most decided and the boldest defender of traducianism. Jerome was a decided advocate of creationism. Augustine, whom we might suppose from his system to have been the most exclusive traducianist, was wrestling with this question all his life. The dominant Church doctrine tended decidedly in favor of Creationism through the influence of Pelagius who availed himself of Creationism to oppose the dogma of inherited sin. The Roman Catholic Church inherited this tendency and maintained the view of Creationism, all the more strongly in proportion to the facility with which it accepted the Semi-Pelagian view as to the corruption of man. In the Roman Church Traducianism has only a few isolated defenders.

In the Lutheran Church the opposition to the Roman Semi-Pelagianism so strongly suggested the traducian view that Creationism was rejected almost as heresy. In the seventeenth century there was left hardly one Lutheran teacher who interested himself in Creationism, but many opposed it by all the means in their power.

Creationism is a view wholly untenable. The proof of the truth of Traducianism is not to be gathered so much from individual passages of Scripture (as perhaps Gen. 46:26; Acts 17:26), but from facts which are equally certified through the whole of Scripture.

These facts are inconsistent with Creationism:

1) The creation of woman; on which account St. Paul says, without any limitation, "the woman is of the man," 1 Cor. 11:8.

2) The sabbath of creation. There is a limit, sharply drawn by God Himself, between His direct creative foundation and His continuous creative control (John 5:17). Of a *creatio continua* in the special sense of the act of creating, Scripture knows nothing. When it is said that God makes our souls (Jer. 38:16; Isa. 57:16), that God's Spirit makes us, and that God forms the spirit within us (Zeb. 12:1; cf. Isa. 51:13), absolutely nothing is proved for Creationism.

3) Inherited sin according to the teaching of Scripture. There subsists between all men and the first created pair who became sinful a close connection, in virtue of which every individual regards the beginning of the human race as his own beginning; so that not only the sin of the race is his sin, but also the transgression of Adam in his transgression, and thus also his guilt.

4) The Incarnation bears an actual testimony against Creationism. Wherever Scripture speaks of Christ in conformity with the human aspect of His personality, it places it under the point of view of begetting, conception, and birth; nowhere of immediate divine creation.

Since Christ, as Son of God, according to His divine nature existed from eternity and in time assumed a human nature into His one person, He is even according to His human nature Son of God, but at the same time He is, in full, absolute truth, Son of Man, the God Man. He has a true human nature, yet without inherited sin, true humanity, for He has all that belongs to the human nature, on the one side "conceived of the Holy Ghost", on the other side "born of a woman." He has human nature (from the Virgin Mary) by the reception of the Holy Ghost and overshadowing of the power of the most High (Luke 1:35)—not only a true body, but also a true human spirit and soul.

Our Dogmaticians rightly say—*Si Christus non assumsisset animam ab anima Mariae, animam humanam non redemisset.*

5) In answer to the principal support of the Creationists, that it is contrary to the dualism of nature and spirit, that the spirit should be able to propagate itself,—we answer, they confound two departments that are sharply distinct.

Scripture teaches us that God is a Spirit, yet it reveals an eternal act of begetting in the Godhead itself (Father and Son), and an eternal procession of the Spirit from God the Father who begets and God the Son who is begotten. Scripture could not speak in this way, if there were not a manner of begetting which corresponds to the nature of spirit.[23]

---

[23] DELITZSCH, Biblical Psychology, pp. 128-142 (condensed).

2

The Original Condition of Man

This topic will be discussed under two heads:
1. The Scripture teaching;
2. The Church doctrine.

Under the Scripture teaching we will treat of nine topics:
1. The idea of man;
2. The meaning of divine image in man;
3. Its psychologic importance;
4. This image lies in the spirit of man;
5. The triplicity of the human spirit;
6. The *nous*, or mind;
7. The *logos*, or word;
8. The spirit of the mind;
9. The primitive state of man.

§ 1. The Scripture Teaching.

The Idea of Man.

The idea of man is expressed in the statement that he is created in the image and after the likeness of God (Gen. 1:26, 27; 5:1; James 3:9; 1 Cor. 11:7). Whatever of this divine image was left in Adam after the Fall, was propagated; for Adam begat a son in his own likeness, after his image (Gen. 5:3). The statement in Gen. 1: 26 ("in our image, after our likeness") does not mean that the divine image is twofold, but likeness refers to the same thing as image, and serves only to fix and strengthen the meaning of image. In fact it is designed to express the thought that the divine image which man bears is really one corresponding- to the original pattern.[24]

The true meaning of the divine image in man:

1) This divine image does not refer to the body, as if the human body were a copy of the divine form, for Elohim, the creative God, is without form. We might say, that the human figure in its nobility was to be so formed that it might serve to represent God Himself when He would reveal Himself (Ps. 94:9, 10).

2) It is equally erroneous to limit the divine likeness to the dominion over the animal world, as the Socinians did. The spiritual dominion of man over the beasts is already indicated in the giving of their names (Gen. 2:19, 20).

---

[24] The patristic and later Roman Catholic exposition attempts to draw an essential distinction between the ideas, image (*tselem*) and likeness (*demuth*), making the former denote the inalienable essence, the latter the likeness to God which was defaced by the Fall. But the two expressions *tselem* and *demuth* are substantially synonymous in Hebrew, and if there is a difference, it is, as Schultz and Oehler observe, simply the difference between the concrete and the abstract.

3) This divine image lies in the spirit of man, for God is Spirit. This divine likeness is to be referred to the whole dignity of man, and lies in his spiritual nature, in virtue of which human nature is sharply distinguished from that of the beasts. Man is designed to hold communion with God, and to be His representative on earth (Oehler). This explains more fully Ps. 8:5, which, referring to the dignity of man, says that he was made a little lower than Elohim, which word stands evidently, as Oehler maintains, as an indefinite and general term for divine being.

Its Psychological Importance.

That man is created in the image of God is a matter of the deepest psychological importance. Delitzsch[25] calls attention to five facts:

1) If man is created in the image of God it follows that the image of God in man refers primarily to his invisible nature;

2) If this divine image is purely spiritual, it can be referred only to the spirit and soul of man, and to his body only so far as the body may be the organ of the life of the spirit and the soul, and be comprehended with them in the unity of human nature;

3) In general, it is not erroneous to regard, with the teachers of the most ancient Church, this image of God as lying in the spiritual, self-conscious and free nature of man,—not in the

---

[25] Biblical Psychology, pp. 79-87.

bodily formation,—not in the dominion over earthly things[26] which is but a manifestation of the divine likeness and not the likeness itself;

4) In one sense there still remains, after the Fall, in all men a trace of this image of God, which is not absolutely lost, but is fearfully marred. There is still a trace of conscience, however crude, some idea of right and wrong, a natural belief in the existence of God, certain intuitive ideas; and in this sense the image of God is incapable of being lost. Man bears in himself and on himself the image of God. Though the divine image is traceable in every child of man, yet it is only perfect in the Second Adam (Heb. 1:3; Col. 1:15; 2 Cor. 4:4), into whose image the believer is being gradually transformed (Col. 3:10; Eph. 4:24; 2 Cor. 3:18)

5) But Scripture passages such as Col. 3:10 and Eph. 4:24 take it for granted that we have lost by the Fall the true image of God. Scripture nowhere says that fallen man possesses the image of God still in living reality, but teaches exactly the reverse. It places the dignity of man as he is now, only in the fact that he is created after the image of God (Gen. 9:6; James 3:9).

This Image of God in Man lies in the Spirit of Man

As man is in the likeness of God and God is a spirit (John 4:24), the first and most special subject of the divine resemblance must lie, therefore, in the spirit of man. If God is Triune, and

---

[26] In this discussion we are especially indebted to Delitzsch Bibl. Psychology, pp. 196-222.

reveals Himself as Father, Son, and Holy Ghost, it follows that in the human spirit there is a triplicity of nature corresponding in some way to the Father, Son, and Holy Ghost, as revealed in the divine Archetype. This is everywhere the Scriptural assumption. It attributes to God the same modes of activity that are proper to the human spirit. Corresponding to the three persons of the Trinity, we can distinguish in the human spirit, the *nous*, the logos, and the *pneuma* of the *nous*, or the mind, the word, and the spirit of the mind. We may thus speak of the triplicity of the human spirit, though we may not succeed in attaining the exact truth in its development.

The Triplicity of the Human Spirit.

If we consider the human spirit, there are three fundamental forms in which its life manifests itself—a striving forwards, a going into itself, and a being still. It strives and longs after the attainment of its destination in God,—it attains in the way of thought to its object,—and then reposes in His nature, as in a continual current of which He is the center. Briefly, the life of the spirit is a threefold unity of will, thought, and experience. We say of experience, for there is a higher spiritual experience, which receives its incitements from the thinking and willing life of the spirit itself; as for example, the peace and joy which are the reflex of the idea of God taken up by the spirit into its thought and will, which idea, in fact, has nothing to do with the nerves of perception.

Of these three distinguishable realities of the life of the spirit,—will and thought and experience,—none comes into operation, none is present in actuality, without the other two being somewhere therein, like to the perichoresis of the three divine acts and of the three divine Persons, who, by virtue of their likeness of nature, invariably penetrate, permeate, and live through one another.

The threefold life of the willing, thinking (word-forming) and experiencing spirit, which points back to the divine archetype, is still man's own in his present natural condition, without being the true primitive divine likeness; for it is only the framework that is left to man of that which has faded away. In the original condition this threefold life of the spirit was a life of love in the likeness of God, filled up by the power of a glad conscience, which knew itself one with God,—an image of the eternally resting flow, and the eternally flowing rest, of blessed life of the Godhead. As God had satisfaction Himself, so the human spirit sought and found satisfaction in God. God was the object of his will, the contents of his thought, the fountain of his experience. In present natural condition, none of the three has the direction and the right contents, but all are fearfully marred, though the triad of spiritual activities and working into each other is nevertheless a shadow of the three acts of the divine life and of the essential perichoresis.

Willing, thinking, and experiencing are thus intimately and closely related. They are predicated of spirit, heart, and soul indiscriminately, in so far as spirit is the supreme principle, the soul the secondary principle, and the heart as the internal focus of the threefold life of man.

It may be said that the spirit of man, in the immediateness of its origin is called breath; in the concentration of its activities, thought and will, heart; and in the sensitive unity of its thought and will, actuated by breath, pervading the heart,—spirit. In the New Testament, especially in the Pauline writings, this psychologic mode of expression is very sharp and profound.

The Nous or Mind.

The human spirit-life is brought to complete development in its three factors of *nous, logos,* and *pneuma* of the *nous* (Eph. 4:23), or mind, word, and spirit of the mind,[27] corresponding to the divine archetype, Father, Logos, and Spirit, the three persons of the Trinity.

That which, or by means of which, the self-conscious spirit thinks and wills, is called *nous* or mind. As all will is an endeavor of the spirit, from the ground of its self-consciousness, towards an object of which it has become conscious, will is thus enclosed on both sides by thought. This is the universal scriptural view.

That the *nous* or mind is both as well the willing as the thinking faculty in man, is seen from the seventh chapter of Romans. When by the divine law man has attained to consciousness about what is good and evil, there begins a conscious will for the good that is known and approved of God. The subject of this will is his *nous*. The moving causes of conduct lie herein, effectuated by the thought (Rom. 14:5). That by virtue of which man thinks and determines himself, the thinking and willing faculty in him, is his *nous*. The invisible things of God are called *nooumena* (Rom. 1:20). They are perceived or understood; that is, man attains by means of his

---

[27] Goeschel: He who observes himself in his thinking, will learn from his own experience to distinguish nous, logos, and pneuma of nous or spirit of the mind (Eph. 4:23).

nous or mind the idea of the Godhead. In Heb. 11:3 also it is stated that the origination of the world by the word of God is a *nooumenon* of faith, that is, of the believing *nous*.

The Logos or Word.

The product of the *nous* or mind is the logos or word; for the human spirit is not endowed merely with consciousness, but with self-consciousness and is therefore a speaking spirit,—a spirit capable of speech. The logos is not only an efficiency of the *nous* but also the organ of the *nous*.

Thought is inward speaking, and speech is audible thinking. Thinking and speaking, spirit and speech, are necessarily associated. Speech is inseparable from thought, for the word is the comprehension of the thought.

Mind and word, in the way of likeness, stand in such essentially necessary relation as do God the Father and God the Son, for if we wish to name the Father in a way corresponding to the Logos, the Son's name, the Father is the *nous*, whereof it is said, Who hath known the mind (noun) of the Lord? (Rom. 11:34; 1 Cor. 2:16). His *nous*, which designed the plan of the universe, is unsearchable. But the Son as Logos is the one eternal self-thought of God,—the thought of His whole proper nature, made objective, independent, and personal in the Word—the Word absolutely—the Word of words. As the Logos is the basis of all other thoughts and words of God, so the Logos is the archetype of the human logos, primarily of the thought of Ego, wherein man becomes objective to himself as a person.

Thoughts, according to a biblical figure, are branches (Job

4:13; 20:2; Ps. 94:19; 139:23), and words are flowers and fruits, which, rooted in the Spirit, and springing from it, blossom and ripen forth through the mouth and lips (Isa. 57:19; Prov. 10:31; 18:20; 12:14; 13:2).

The Spirit of the Mind.

The *nous* or mind or human understanding, thinking in all directions, comes to the word and by the word it advances further. It meditates, and breaks forth, as it were, out of the chrysalis, and attains to form and shape in the thought—invested in the word. The word is the means, the organ, the conditioning of the thought; the expression of all will and thought.

But the third and final stage is that in which words are at an end, where the spirit, although in a more realized sense, is again in thought, as in the beginning before the birth of the word.

For the thought and will, which serve to develop the spirit, and find their expression in the word, cease without a word: the crown of the word is the spirit without the word,—the innermost sanctuary of the heart. This is what the apostle means in Eph. 4:23 by *pneuma* of the *nous*, spirit of the mind—"be ye renewed in the spirit of your mind."

There is thus not only a mind, which according to its nature belongs to the *pneuma* or spirit, and in the natural man is mind of the flesh (Col. 2:18) instead of mind of the spirit but, moreover, a spirit also, which, according to its nature, belongs to the *nous*, or mind, and is therefore inversely called spirit of the mind.

THE ORIGINAL CONDITION OF MAN

What kind of a spirit this is, is to be gathered—although this has escaped the commentators—from 1 Cor. 14:14, 15, 19; for the apostle speaking of the speech with tongues, distinguishes between a human spirit and the human *nous* or understanding.

The apostle calls the region of immediate experience and intuition, the *pneuma* or spirit, as distinct from the *nous* (mind or understanding) of man.

It is the spirit in the narrower sense (distinguished from *pneuma* in a wider sense as 1 Cor. 5:3; 7:34; 2 Cor. 7:1) as experiencing, and especially as seeing with immediate intuition—which is the image of the divine Holy Spirit.

Since the fall the *nous* has become the mind of the flesh, the thought and will are determined by the flesh (Eph. 2:3); and the *pneuma* or spirit of man, in its God resembling nature, glowing and panting with love (1 Thess. 5:19; Rom. 12:11; Acts 18:25), is, as it were, extinct and dead. The true nature of the *pneuma* is not indeed destroyed, but it is buried beneath a tendency which contradicts it.

Therefore man needs to be renewed in the spirit of the mind (Eph. 4:20-24). The renewal seeks to make the *nous* or mind spiritual again, which has become fleshly, and therefore lays hold of the spirit of the mind, which, instead of being penetrated by the Holy Spirit, whose image it is, is possessed by the spirit of this world.

This spirit of the mind is the secret spring whence the *nous* or mind receives its impulses, which it adopts into consciousness and translates into acts of will.

In this *pneuma* of the *nous*, this spirit of the mind, is the standing- place of the peace of God, which surpasses all *nous* (understanding) (Phil. 4:7); here is the bottom of all ethically profound experience (Mark 8:12; John 11:33; 13:21); here is the sanctuary of all immediate communion of God and man, and the seat where conscience has its home.

In Scripture, this innermost threefold personal life of *nous*, logos, and *pneuma* of *nous*, or mind, word, and spirit of the mind, is called the inner man (Rom. 7:22; 2 Cor. 4:16; Eph. 3:16); and in reference to the unity of its origin, its seat and home, the hidden man of the heart (1 Pet. 3:4).

These ideas do not belong exclusively, as does the new man to the life of regeneration, for every man still has an inward nature; but in the natural man this inward nature is estranged from its true being, although the features of the divine archetype are still recognizable therein.

The Primitive State of Man.

The constitution of man in his primitive state we learn partly from the second chapter of Genesis, and partly by arguing backward from the change occasioned by sin. We would emphasize three points:

1. Innocence and childlike intercourse with God;
2. Harmonious relation to nature;
3. Conditional exemption from death.

1) Man was created good (Gen. 1:31), that is, conformed to the divine aim. But this good must be developed into free self-determination. The conception of the original state as a created condition of wisdom and sanctity contradicts the statement in Genesis; it would be much more in the sense of the Old Testament to say, as Eccles. 7:29 expresses it: "God made man upright" (*yashar*, right).

The view that the original state was only an absence of

actual sin, in the sense of a state of pure indifference, or a state in which evil was already latent, so that in the Fall the disposition which already existed in man only came forth, is equally irreconcilable with Genesis.

2) In the primitive condition, man lives in undisturbed and peaceful union with nature and with God. The latter is made especially clear by the contrast implied in Gen. 3:8. The peaceful relation of man with nature is taught partly in the description of the life in Paradise in general, and partly in the contrast between the present relation of man to nature and his condition before sin, since man must now make nature of service to him by toiling and struggling (Gen. 3:17, 18; 5:29), and since he exercises his dominion over the animals by deeds of violence and destruction of life (Gen. 9:2, 3 contrasted with Gen. 1:29). Hence prophecy has depicted the termination of this hostile relation in its description of the time of salvation (in the well-known passages, Isa. 11:6-8; 65:25).

3) Lastly, in Gen. 2, immortality is ascribed to man, but conditionally, in the sense of to be able not to die (*posse non mori*). This idea, indeed, does not necessarily lie in the words of Gen. 2:17, "in the day that thou eatest thereof thou shalt surely die," but it is quite clear from 3:22 that the possibility of reaching immortality was annexed to the life in Paradise, and that immortality was destined for man so far as he should live in unbroken communion with God.

§ 2. The Church Doctrine.

The Greek Fathers.

The form of expression in Gen. 1:27 has been always employed by the Church. According to Clement of Alexandria (died about 220) man is the most beautiful hymn to the praise of the Deity, a heavenly plant, and, generally speaking, the principal object of the love of God. Some of the Alexandrian theologians taught that man had been created, not so much after the image of God Himself, as after the image of the Logos, an image after an image. But all admitted that the image of God in man had a special reference to the spiritual endowments of man. The more spiritual view was, that the life of the soul, partaking of the divine nature, shines through the physical organism, and is reflected especially in the countenance and looks of man. Origen (died 254) refers the divine image exclusively to the spirit of man. Iranaeus (202), and especially Clement and Origen in their acumen, began to make an arbitrary distinction between *tselem* (image) and *demuth* (likeness) . Neander sees in this "the first germ of the distinction, afterward so important, between the *dona naturalia* and *supernaturalia*" emphasized so strongly by the later Roman Catholic Church.

Theophilus (d. 181) starts the question: Was Adam created with a mortal or immortal nature? and replies: Neither the one nor the other, but he was fitted for either, receiving immortality as a reward if he aspired after it by obeying the divine commandments, and becoming the author of his own ruin if he disobeyed God.

The Latin Fathers.

The Latin Fathers did not agree in their opinions respecting the image of God, though most of them admitted that it consisted in reason imparted to man, in his capacity of knowing God, and in his dominion over the irrational creation. The Semipelagians Gennadius (d. 471) and Faustus (d. 492), made a distinction between imago and likeness. Gregory the Great (d. 604) regards the image of God in which man was created, as lost by the Fall. The immortality of the soul was universally believed.

The Scholastics.

Most of the theologians of this period adhered to the distinction between *tselem* (image) and *demuth* (likeness), drawn by some of the Greek Fathers. In this respect the views of Peter Lombard (d. 1164) are very important. He divides the endowments of the first man into *dona naturalia*, the image of God, what man had in *donum superadditum* his original natural constitution; and *dona gratiae*, the likeness of God, which were added to his original constitution. The image, the *dona naturae* he makes to consist in purity and vigor of all the powers of the soul. The original righteousness was added to the *dona pura naturalia* as a *donum superadditum*, and consisted in the likeness of God. When man lost this last by sin, no important alteration took place in his nature.

Bonaventura (d. 1274) also distinguishes between the image and likeness of God in man, making the former consist in the intellectual qualities, the latter in those of the disposition or the heart, by virtue of which alone communion with God can be realized .

Roman Catholicism.

The theologians of the Roman Catholic Church agreed with the majority of the Scholastics in distinguishing between the image and the likeness of God. The former alone belonged to man's nature at his creation. Original righteousness, the likeness of God, was not a natural endowment, not an element belonging to man's nature, but a supernatural gift of special grace, which man has now lost through the Fall. The *donum superadditum* did not inwardly and personally belong to man. This is the doctrine taught in the Roman Catechism and fully developed by Bellarmine and their later dogmaticians.

Teaching of Luther.

Luther, and Protestantism in general, maintained that God created man in the possession of perfect righteousness and holiness, qualities which, together with immortality, belonged to his original nature.

Luther finds the image of God in man, not so much in his general spiritual endowment, the powers of thought, will, etc.,—which have remained since the Fall, and in which Satan far excels us—but in the RIGHT WILL (*recta voluntas*), a will entirely pure morally, and entirely devoted to the love of God and fellowman, and in a true and unerring knowledge of God. The native powers of Adam were in an excellent and faultless condition, whereas they now are ruined and most thoroughly enfeebled. His dominion over external nature was regarded as also constituting a feature of the divine image. Briefly stated "Man was immersed in that which was good, and without any evil lust, just as God Himself, so that he was lull of God."[28]

Lutheran Confessions.

Among the Lutheran Symbols, the Augsburg Confession passes by the primitive state of man, but the doctrine is contained in the Apology[29] (79:18-20): "Man was fashioned in the image and likeness of God (Gen. 1:27). What else is this than that, in man, there, were embodied such wisdom and righteousness, as apprehended God, and in which God was reflected? That is, to man there were given the gifts of the knowledge of God, the fear of God, confidence in God, and the like . . . And Paul shows in Eph. 5:9 and Col. 3:10, that the image of God is the knowledge of God, righteousness, and truth.

Our Lutheran Dogmaticians.

1) Calovius: It is called a state of integrity, because man in it was upright and incorrupt (Eccl. 7:29) in intellect, will, the corporeal affections and endowments, and in all things was perfect. They call it also the state of innocence, because he was innocent and holy, free from sin and pollution.

---

[28] See Koestlin, The Theology of Luther. 2 Vols. Index.
[29] Jacobs: Book of Concord. People's Edition. Index. 1911.

2) Of the words *tselem* and *demuth*, Hollaz says: These words are not expressions for different things, as if image denoted the very substance of the human soul, and likeness its accidental perfections or attributes (as some of the Papists say), but likeness is exegetical of image, thus designating the image as most like or very similar.

3) Quenstedt: The image of God, specifically understood, is not to be sought for in those things which yet remain in man since the Fall, and which are truly in man unregenerate . . . The image of God is a natural perfection, consisting in an entire conformity with wisdom, justice, immortality, and majesty of God, which was divinely concreated in the first man, in order that he might perfectly know, love, and glorify God, his Creator.

4) God bestowed a certain wisdom or perfection of intellect. Proof is given by Quenstedt:

a) From Col. 3:9, 10;

b) Appropriate application of names by Adam, Gen. 2:19;

c) Adam's recognition of Eve, Gen. 2:23;

d) Prediction of the perpetuity of the conjugal relation, Gen. 2:24.

And he adds: This knowledge of Adam was finite and limited, and could have been perfected more and more, both by revelation and by his own experience and observation.

5) Man had holiness and freedom of the will, and possessed the power to live in conformity with the will of God.

Quenstedt: This perfection of will consisted in

a) a natural inclination to that which is good;

b) a free and unhindered volition of good;

c) the execution of that volition;

d) but holiness in the first man did not introduce absolute

impeccability, but only a relative freedom from sin in his will.

6) Man possessed purity of the natural affections, and the perfect harmony of all his powers and impulses.

Hollaz: For reason promptly obeyed the divine law; the will, reason; the sensuous appetite, the will; the affections, the appetite; and the members of the body, the affections.

7) These spiritual and moral excellencies, this original righteousness, is called the image of God. Calovius:

a) It is called righteousness, both in respect to its essence, for by its own nature it was true, perfect, right, sound, and incorrupt, and also in respect to its efficiency because it made man righteous in the sight of God, that is, innocent, acceptable, and holy.

b) Righteousness is called original, because it was first of all in man, created in his mind, of perfect holiness and purity, distinguished from moral, imputed, imperfect righteousness, and from every other kind whatsoever.

8) As natural consequences of these spiritual excellencies three corporeal excellencies are connected, impassibility, immortality, and dominion.

a) Impassibility. Hollaz: Painful and destructive sufferings are the punishment of sin (Gen. 3:16); wherefore the first man, being without sin, was free from its bitter suffering.

b) Immortality. Quenstedt proves this from Gen. 2:17; Rom. 5:12; 6:23.

It is one thing not to be able to die, and another to be able not to die, and still another not to be able not die. The last belongs to all sinners, the second to Adam in his state of integrity, and the first to the blessed in heaven.

c) Dominion. The exalted dignity of the likeness to God manifested itself also in external dominion over the other animals (Gen. 1:26-28).

9) The original condition of man, therefore, is called a most happy one.

Quenstedt: The happiness of it appeared

a) from the condition of the soul, which was and holy;

b) from the condition of the body, which was beautiful, not susceptible of suffering, and immortal;

c) from the condition of life, which was happy and blessed;

d) from the condition of his habitation, which was most pleasant, truly a garden of pleasure, called Paradise.

10) This divine image was thus a natural endowment, and not an external, supernatural, and supplementary gift, as the Roman Catholic Church teaches. If original righteousness were said to be a superadded gift, this would conflict with Gen. 1:31.

Arminianism.

The Arminian Symbols agree in insisting on the original freedom of the will, but reject on this very account the notion of a primitive state of perfect holiness, because if there had been such, man could not have sinned. Limhorch maintains that the state of innocence of our first parents to which so much importance is attached, must have been united with ignorance, otherwise they would have known that serpents cannot speak, and would have been led to suspect something wrong.

Socinianism.

According to the Socinians the divine image in man consists especially in his dominion over nature, including mind and reason. Man was not created perfect or originally endowed with a high measure of wisdom, nor with immortality, and therefore did not lose this virtue by the law. He had a negative or possible free will, not a positive actual freedom.

Rationalism (including Semi-Pelagianism and Pelagianism).

According to Pelagians and Rationalism man was created a rational free agent, but without moral character. He was neither righteous nor unrighteous, holy nor unholy. He could become either. All who hold this view reject the doctrine of original righteousness as irrational.

The second distinguishing feature of the Pelagian or Rationalistic doctrine as to man's original state, is that man was created mortal,—that Adam was liable to death, and certainly would have died in virtue of the original constitution of his nature.

We answer that it is expressly stated in Scripture that death is the wages of sin (Rom. 6:23), and the consequence of Adam's sin (Gen. 2:17; 3:19; Rom. 5:12; 1Cor. 15:21); and it is plainly implied in Gen. 2:17 that if he did not eat he should not die. Probably Luther was right, when he thought that the effect of the fruit of the tree of life of which our first parents would have been permitted to eat had they not sinned, would have been to preserve their bodies in perpetual youth.

The Theory of Speculative Theologians.

Some speculative theologians as Schleiermacher, Nitzsch, Julius Mueller, Hofmann and others, deny that any positive determination to virtue inhered originally in man's nature, and regard man at the beginning as simply possessed of spiritual powers, including mainly personality, that is, self-consciousness and self-determination.

Modern Scientific Theories.

Most of our modern scientists claim that man's prehistoric condition was one of primitive savagery and utter barbarism.

We answer: This theory rests on insufficient fact as a basis of induction. In the earliest times of which we have any record, we find nations in a high state of civilization, and Strong correctly remarks, "the subsequent progress has been downward, and no nation is known to have recovered from barbarism except as the result of influence from without." Had savagery been man's primitive condition, he never could have emerged. Civilization can only be kept alive by a power genuinely Christian. There is degeneration in all the organic orders. Very early races have a purer faith than the later ones. The universal tradition of a golden age of happiness is best explained by the Scripture view and a subsequent apostasy.

3

The Fall

The Divisions.

The fact of sin, a fact established by universal experience, proves that man converted the possibility of apostasy from God into actuality, and thus confirms the Scripture account.

We follow the arrangement of Luthardt and discuss the topic under four heads:
1) The Biblical account;
2) The historical actuality of the Fall;
3) The teaching of the dogmaticians;
4) Attempts to explain away the historical facts.

§ 1. The Biblical Account.

The Scripture Narrative.

In the third chapter of Genesis we have the divine account of the Fall. There is not the slightest hint in the narrative itself that it is not to be taken as historical. In the New Testament it is acknowledged as historical and used as such. The New Testament asserts that "through one man sin entered into the world, and death through sin" (Rom. 5:12); that "the serpent beguiled Eve in his craftiness" (2 Cor. 11:3); that "Adam was not beguiled, but the woman being beguiled fell into transgression" (1 Tim. 2:14).

In Gen. 3 the Fall is described as it appeared outwardly. The serpent is the apparent agent of the temptation, yet the account is not without hints of those deeper causes which lay beneath the surface. The historical fact of the Fall finds its essential confirmation in the perpetual occurrence of sin.

The Importance and Magnitude of the Fall.

This does not reveal itself in the mere outward facts, which apart from the moral connections might seem insignificant, but it turns upon the perversion of the internal personal relation to God, a perversion which consummated and revealed itself in the Fall. This change of relation shows itself in the shame and fear which at the same time testified to the consciousness of guilt. That shame and fear are confirmed by the divine words of reproof, even upon the serpent, which is to remain forever a living symbol of the temptation that wrought the Fall, and of the malignant poison of sin and of the degradation that follows. The magnitude of the Fall is revealed in the very greatness of the divine word of promise which was given of God in order to awaken penitence and faith in the heart of man.

§ 2. The Historical Actuality of the Fall.

The Historical Actuality of the Fall.

That Gen. 3 is historical, that some such event as is there detailed must have occurred, is clear from the necessity of accounting for the rise of evil within mankind. Some such occurrence, the result of some free act yet with its incentives from without, must have taken place at the beginning of the history of the race.

The heathen traditions, even with their perversions, give a certain confirmation of the Bible narrative.

The Tree of Knowledge.

According to Augustine and the best theologians in general, the tree of knowledge was not in itself pernicious, but only a means of testing obedience, and of moral development. It served merely as a moral test. The choice may have been purely arbitrary, and perhaps some other tree might have answered as well as the one actually chosen, yet we may conjecture that this one was preeminent in beauty and attractions, in the center of the garden, presenting the outward appearance at least of being no less adapted for good than the other trees of the garden (Gen. 3:6).

Delitzsch on Gen. 3:6.

Delitzsch remarks: Among the trees of Paradise there is one behind which death is lurking, and this one is forbidden to man, that he may not fall a prey to the power of death, but conquer it by obedience to God. It was possible for man to remain in the happy condition in which he was created, and to establish it by submission of his own to the Divine will. But it was also possible that this subordination to God should be as such repulsive to him, and that he should entirely, and of his own accord, rebelliously assert his ego against the Divine (as Satan did). It was possible, also, in the third place, that, tempted from without by an already existing power of evil, he should lose sight of the Divine will, and seduced by the charm of the forbidden, fall into disobedience. This last possibility, comparatively less evil than the second one, was realized. He was tempted from without, and fell.

The True Cause of the Fall and its Results.

The eating of the fruit of the tree of knowledge was the occasion rather than the proper cause of the results that ensued. The fall was not in eating but took place before it. Man did not fall because he ate, but he ate because he fell.

Augustine says: "Wherefore was it prohibited except that it might be shown that obedience itself (per se) is good and that disobedience in itself (per se) is evil."

Lessons Drawn from Gen. 3.

A careful study of Gen. 3:1-7 teaches us:

1) The woman shows herself fully conscious of the divine prohibition, and of the penalty with which its transgression is threatened;

2) Her confidence in God began to waver at Satan's first attempt to excite her mistrust, and she did not flee at his first utterance;

3) When Satan practically charges God 1) with falsehood, and 2) with envy, the woman begins to doubt and ambition begins to rise in her mind;

4) Thus doubt, unbelief, and pride were the roots of the sin of our first parents, as they have been of all the sins of their posterity;

5) It is evident from the narrative that Adam and Eve ate together of the forbidden fruit. The behavior of Adam, whether he was present throughout the whole scene or not, is throughout extraordinary. In the New Testament Adam is distinctly regarded as the chief transgressor (Rom. 5:12; 1 Cor. 15:21, 22). The woman was deceived, but man was persuaded. What Adam did, he did of his own choice and with open eyes.

6) The progress brought to pass by partaking of the tree of knowledge of good and evil, the taste of sin and its guilt and the punishment of death, is the exact opposite to the progress which, according to the purpose of God, was to have been brought about by abstaining therefrom, even their confirmation of the good, and eternal life.

7) The minds of our first parents were awakened and enlarged, but the price they had paid for it was their innocence and peace. The feeling of shame and guilt was but the

beginning of the evil consequences of sin.

The Serpent.

The serpent was the tool of the Evil Spirit, the organ of Satan. There was a fall in the higher spiritual world before the fall of man; and this is not only plainly taught in 2 Pet. 2:4 and Jude 6, but is assumed in everything, that the Scriptures say of Satan,—who from this circumstance is commonly styled in Scripture "the serpent" (Rev. 12:14, 15), "the old serpent" (Rev. 12:9; 20:2), "the great red dragon" (Rev. 12:3, 7, 9, 13, etc.). The literal truth of this narrative is attested by Christ, and his apostles (John 8:44; 2 Cor. 11:3; Rom. 16:20; Rev. 12:9; 20:2).

Augustine truly says: In the serpent, the Devil himself spake, using it as an organ.

§ 3. The Dogmatic Statement of the Doctrine.

Our earlier Dogmaticians.

Sin itself, the essence of the deed, is a falling away from moral fellowship with God.

Hollaz defines the sin of the first man as: "A transgression of the law of Paradise, whereby our first parents, having been persuaded by the devil, and having abused the freedom of the will, violated the divine prohibition concerning the not eating the fruit of the tree of the knowledge of good and evil, and brought down upon themselves and their posterity; the divine image having been lost, a great guilt, and the liability to temporal and eternal punishment." . . . "Our first parents, by their, fall immediately violated the positive law given in Paradise, mediately and virtually by their disobedience they broke down the bars of the entire moral law." . . .

"The sin formally consists in deflection from the positive law of God. This lawlessness involves acts sin,—in the intellect, unbelief; in the will, aversion to God; in the affection and appetite, inordinate longing for that which God has prohibited; and in the act and deed, positive transgression."

Testimony of Delitzsch.

1) There is a vast difference between the sin of our first parents and the sin by which Satan became Satan.

2) When Scripture speaks of Satan, we always see in him, although he is compelled to serve God, the enemy of God as such, and of godly-minded people as such.

3) He behaves as if he were God (Matt. 4:8, 9); and in some measure, moreover, he is the god of this world (2 Cor. 4:4).

4) His sin was and still is revolt against God,—striving to surpass His glory.

5) With the Fathers we have to conceive of his sin and his overthrow according to scriptural statement such as Isa. 14:12-15.

The sin of man can certainly rise to the Satanic, and the primal sin of man had much in common with the primal sin of Satan.

1) Yet in its beginning, although it is revolt, it is not direct revolt against the person of God, but indirect, arraying itself against God's commands.

2) It is not enmity towards God and hatred of Him, but apostasy from God by attachment to the world,—a falling from God to a falling to the world.

3) It is not the warfare directly turned against God; but a breaking by self-will of the limits set by Him, and the consequent sinking away from His communion.

4) It was selfishness opposed to God,—without God an idolatrous and atheistic selfishness.

Briefly to draw the distinction:

The primal sin of Satan was a direct, purely spiritual revolt against God;

The primal sin of man was indirect revolt corporeally effected against God, brought about by means of a masked power of deceit coming from without ("beguiled", Gen. 3:13. 2 Cor. 11:3; 1 Tim. 2:14), and by the super-added material and sensual attraction of the forbidden tree.

§ 4. Attempts to Explain Away Historical Facts.

Allegory or Myth.

Modern criticism, of course, has not left untouched so important a doctrine as that of the Fall. Various attempts have been made to explain it away.

Some have acknowledged the fact of the fall, but have treated as allegorizing the narrative of the way in which it is recorded. Even in the ancient church there were explanations of this class. Clement Alexandrinus, Origen and others, following Philo, regarded the fall as originating in sensual lust.

Philosophy.

Others regarded it as a philosophical explanation of man's rising to the experience of free reason. The Ophites or serpent-worshipers regarded the fall as the breaking through of the bonds of Jaldabaoth, and the serpent was worshiped as the incarnate wisdom. A curious illustration of the way in which seeming extremes meet is found in the fact that a similar thought has been expressed by modern writers in the modern way,—the fall being considered as the dawn of reason, the happiest event in the history of the race. Hegel says: "the condition of innocence, the condition of Paradise, is a park where only animals and not man can remain. For the beast is in union with God, but only by itself. Only man is spirit, that is, for himself. This being for himself, this independence, this self-consciousness, is however at the same time the separation from the Universal Divine Spirit. The Fall is consequently the eternal myth of man, that very thing whereby he becomes man."

Strauss most completely states this mode of thinking. "God could not have given such a command. God, the primal spirit, could only have conducted himself like spirit and liberally toward the human spirit, which was created after his image. Only a brutal subaltern, who would find pleasure in treating his subjects imperiously could have given such a command."

Hase considers the narrative as but "an image of what takes place in every man", and Nitzsch regards it as "a true history, but not an actual one."

The Account is Historical.

All these theories at once fall before the majesty of God's Word, nor do they commend themselves to sound reason. They solve no mystery, they rest on no facts. They are simple escapes of defiant or of unconscious unbelief. The spirit and method of interpretation by which they are reached would overthrow all sacred history and all divine doctrine. A historical redemption provided by a real Savior must rest upon a historical cause. Sacred history is a unity. Its earlier part conditions its later part. It stands or falls together.

The following reasons are generally given in favor of the historicity of the narrative.

1) There is no intimation in the account itself that it is not historical;

2) The narrative occurs in a historical book;

3) Scripture everywhere regards it as veritable history, even in its details;

4) The incidents of the narrative are suitable to man's condition of innocent but untried state;

5) The analogy of faith demands it.

4

Original Sin

The Divisions.

The universality of sin proves the hereditary transmission of it from those who at the beginning fell into sin. From our first parents sin passed into the whole human race which springs from them, and in this race exists a moral corruption which consists in the loss of the original righteousness and in the dominion of a tendency of the will in conflict with God, in which is involved guilt.

This whole subject will be discussed under three heads:[30]

1) The Scripture doctrine;
2) The Church doctrine;
3) Modern criticism.

---

[30] See LUTHARDT, Kompendium der Dogmatik, § 41.

§ 1. The Scripture Doctrine.

The Old Testament.

The universality of sin is presupposed alike in the Old Testament and in the New. See 1 Kings 8:46, "There is no man that sinneth not" (2 Chron. 6:36); Job 14:4, "Who can bring a clean thing out of an unclean? not one"; Ps. 14:3, "There is none that doeth good, no, not one"; 143:2, "For in thy sight shall no man living be justified"; Prov. 20:9, "Who can say, I have made my heart clean, I am pure from my sin?"; Eccl. 7:20, "Surely there is not a righteous man upon earth, that doeth good, and sinneth not".

The entire institution of sacrifice implies the guilt of all men. Circumcision symbolically expressed the corruption which clings to every man.

The New Testament.

Matt. 7:11 speaks of all men as "being evil"; in Rom. 3:23 Paul affirms that "all have sinned, and fall short of the glory of God", and in 1 John 1:10 the Apostle declares "if we say that we have not sinned, we make him a liar, and his word is not in us", and in 1 John 1:8 "if we say that we have no sin, we deceive ourselves, and the truth is not in us", and in 1 John 5:19 he adds "the whole world lieth in the evil one".

The universal necessity of redemption, and the universality of its aim, are proof of universal corruption.

The Unity of the Teaching of Scripture.

Original sin, according to the view both of the Old and New Testaments, has its root in the very beginning of the individual life, that is, of the very nature of man. Gen. 6:3 (R. V. marg.) "in their going astray they are flesh"; 8:21 "the imagination of man's heart is evil from youth;" Ps. 51:5 "I was shapen in iniquity; and in did my mother conceive me"; Matt. 15:19 "For out the heart come forth evil thoughts, murders, adulteries, thefts, false witness, railings"; John 3:6 which is born of the flesh is flesh"; Rom. 5: 12-14 through one man sin entered into the world, and death sin; and so death passed unto all men, for that all sinned"; Rom. 7:7-11.

Consequently men are "by nature children of wrath" (Eph. 2:3), are "guilty before God" (Rom. 3:19; 5:16, 18, 19), and consequently under death (Rom. 5:12-14).

§ 2. The Church Doctrine.

The Greek Church.

The Greek Church acknowledges, indeed, the universality of sin, but fails in the profounder knowledge of sin in general, and especially fails in the distinct recognition of its hereditary connection with the act of Adam. This arose from the great emphasis laid by the Greek Church upon the freedom of the will, in consequence of the controversies with the Gnostics.

The Early Greek Fathers.

Justin Martyr complained of the universality of sin. The whole human race is under the curse; for cursed is everyone who does not keep the law. He attributes the fall mainly to the cunning malignity of Satan, but man added credulity and disobedience. Nevertheless original sin and the imputation of Adam's guilt are conceptions foreign to him. Every man deserves death, because in his disobedience he is like the first man.

Clement of Alexandria directs our attention to the internal conflict which sin has introduced into the nature of man. It does not form a part of our nature but nevertheless it is spread through the whole human race. The sinning is engrafted, and common to all, though he attributes this to the infirmity of finite human nature. We come to sin without ourselves knowing how. Man now stands in the same relation to the tempter in which Adam stood prior to the fall. Clemens indeed admits the universality of sin among men, but he did not consider man as absolutely depraved. He most strongly rejects the idea of imputing original sin to children.

Origen also conceives of sin as a universal corruption, since the world is apostate, but with him moral evil was mainly something negative. Origen thought that souls were stained with sin in a former state, and thus enter into the world in a sinful condition. He also added the idea, allied to the notions of the Gnostics and Manicheans, that there is a stain in physical generation itself. By insisting upon the freedom of the human will, he is in strong contrast with Augustine. He also maintains that concupiscence is not reckoned as sin so long as it has not ripened into a purpose. Subsequent times, especially after Jerome, have seen in Origen the precursor of Pelagius and

Pelagianism.

The Later Greek Fathers

The Early Greek Fathers do not express so strong a sense of sin as do those of the later period general they agree both in seeking the source of sin in the human will and in clearing God from all responsibility.

Athanasius regarded sin as something negative, and believed it to consist in the blindness and indolence of man, which prevent him from elevating himself to God. Indolence is allied with sensuality, because it clings to what is nearest, the bodily and the visible.

Even this lather of orthodoxy maintained that man has the ability of choosing good as well as evil. He also allowed exceptions from original sin, notably in the case of Jeremiah and John the Baptist, who were born prior to the appearance of Christ. Nevertheless, death has reigned even over them who have not sinned alter the similitude of Adam's transgression (Rom. 5:14).

Gregory of Nazianzus (d. 390) held that the sin of Adam was followed by disastrous effects upon the human race, but restricted these evils to the mortality of the body and the hardships and miseries of life. He admitted also that the moral powers of man had been enfeebled by the fall, but was far from asserting the total depravity of mankind and the entire loss of free will. Ullmann maintains that "Gregory by no means taught doctrines afterwards propounded by Pelagius and his followers; but if all his sentiments be duly considered, it will be found that he is far more a Pelagian than an Augustinian." Yet it must not be forgotten that Augustine appealed to Gregory in preference to all other Greek Fathers.

Chrysostom (d. 407), whose whole tendency was of a practical and moral kind, insisted most of all upon the liberty of man and his moral self-determination, and censured those who endeavored to excuse their own defects by ascribing the origin of sin to the fall of Adam. His practical sphere of labor in the cities of Antioch and Constantinople gave a still greater impulse to this tendency. But Chrysostom, in opposition to a false moral pride, urged quite as strongly the existence of depravity.

The Western Church.

The connection of the two, Adam's sin and original sin, was recognized in a more decided form in the Western Church. Both death and physical evils were considered as the effects of Adam's sin. But in the early period, opinions concerning the moral depravity of each individual and the sin of the race in general were not as yet fully developed. They were so inclined to look upon sin as the free act of man's will, that they could hardly conceive of it as simply a hereditary tendency, transmitted from one to another. The sin of every individual, as found his experience, had its type in the sin of Adam, and consequently appeared to be a repetition of the first sin rather than its necessary consequence.

The Latin Fathers before Augustine.

Irenaeus (d. 202; after 178, bishop of Lyons in France) gives us more profound views about the effects of the fall, and has so fully developed the doctrine of original sin and hereditary evil, that according to Duncker, "the characteristic features of the western type of doctrine may be distinctly recognized". He asserts that man, freely yielding to the voice of the tempter, has become a child, disciple, and servant of the devil. He also thinks that in consequence of the sin of Adam, men are already in a state of guilt. He says: "The consequences of the sin of Adam stretch themselves over his entire posterity;" "as we have sinned in Adam, we die in Adam, in order to be redeemed to life in Christ."

Tertullian (d. 220) teaches that sin is propagated as completely as the soul and, body. The phrase *vitium originis*, first used by him, is in perfect accordance with this view. But he did not consider inherent depravity, as constituting accountability, nor did he believe in the entire absence of human liberty. He was far from imputing original sin to children as real sin, but on his own basis of propagation of sin, his objection to infant baptism falls. Compare his saying, "Every soul is counted in Adam, until it is counted again in Christ, and is impure until it is recounted".

Cyprian (d. 258) held that man lost by the fall the higher physical strength along with immortality. He acknowledges inherent depravity, and defends infant baptism on this ground; baptism serving, however, only to purify infants from a foreign guilt which is imputed to them, not from any guilt which is properly their own. He says: "There were also before Christ noble men, but they were not without the original and personal fault, conceived and born in sins."

Ambrose (d. at Milan, 397) taught the defilement of sin by birth and appealed especially to Ps. 51:5 in support of original sin, but without determining to what extent every individual shares in the common guilt. He did not exclude the liberty of man from the work of moral reformation. He says, "We all are born under sin; we whose very origin is in a vitiated condition." He teaches the hereditary transmission of guilt. "We all have sinned in the first man, and through the succession of nature, the succession of culpability has also been transmitted from one upon all." On Rom. 5 he says: "It is manifest that in Adam all sinned, as it were, in the mass, for he being corrupted through sin, all whom he begat are born in sin. From him therefore we are all sinners, because from him we all are." In his exposition on Luke 7 he says: "Adam was and in him we all were; Adam perished and in him we all perished."

Augustine.

Augustine (d. 430),—one of the deepest theologians of all ages, and the greatest, it can well be said, among the Church Fathers, by whose side, in fullness and depth of thought and grandeur of character, a Luther alone can stand, carried out still further this doctrine of original sin, in the most valuable of his voluminous writings, his Anti-Pelagian works.

With his profound conceptions Augustine considered the human race as a compact mass, a collective body, responsible in its unity and solidarity.

"By propagation sin passed from the first man to others, and thus every one participated in original sin, the vice of origin; for nature and the vice of nature are simultaneously propagated."

Hence also he infers universal condemnation, extending even to infants.

He says: "The infant is punished by perdition, because it belongs to the mass of perdition."

He allows indeed "that sin cannot be without will;" but he holds that the will is responsible in its condition as well as in its acts; that sin is connected with a depraved will before that will goes forth in acts. He builds upon the Old Latin translation of Rom. 5:12, the *"in quo,"* in whom all sinned, and says: we were all in that one, since we all were that one".

Carrying out his system in all its logical consequences, he laid down the following proposition as his doctrine: "As all men have sinned in Adam, they justly subject to the condemnation of God on account of this hereditary sin and the guilt thereof". He was also the first who strongly emphasized the imputation of original sin.

Pelagius and Celestius.

Augustine perceives no other difference between Pelagius and Celestius than that the latter was more open, the former more guarded, the latter more obstinate, the former more deceitful, or, to say the least, that the latter was more straightforward, the former more cunning.

The views which these two held were partly in accordance with the opinions hitherto entertained by the theologians of the Greek Church, but in part carried to a much greater length in the denial of natural depravity.

Augustine has preserved the seven propositions of which the

Pelagians were accused at the synod of Carthage (412), but we must not forget that what is commonly called Pelagianism does not so much represent the single notions of a single individual, as a complete moral and religious system, which formed a decided contrast to Augustinianism.

Pelagianism was directly opposed to the doctrine of Scripture, especially to the teachings of Paul, and the general belief of the Church, and thus threatened the fundamental doctrines of the Gospel. In particular the seven propositions of the Pelagians were as follows:

1. Adam was a created mortal, so that he would have died whether he had sinned or not;

2. Adam's sin injured only himself, and not the human race;

3. Newborn infants are in the same condition in which Adam was previous to the fall;

4. Neither does the whole human race die in consequence of Adam's death or transgression, nor does it rise from the dead in consequence of Christ's resurrection;

5. Infants obtain eternal life, though they be not baptized;

6. The law is as good a means of salvation as the gospel;

7. There were some men, even before the appearance of Christ, who did not commit sin.

"There is," says Pelagius, "in our souls a certain natural sanctity, if I may so speak. That first sin come (to the human race, not by propagation, but by example."

In the Pelagian system the individual is falsely isolated from the connection of the race. Nothing is more manifest than that the human race has morally a race character, as natural to it as the faculties of the mind, the organs of the body; indeed in some sense more so, for the, generic moral nature of man has not the divine range either the intellect or the body.

Pelagius supposes the Grace of God to be something external and added to the efforts put forth by the free will of man. He attached great importance to the power of the natural man to choose between good and evil. This is the determining and fundamental conception in his doctrine of sin and grace, and freedom of the will is the absolute capacity of choice to determine equally for good or evil. Julius Mueller justly remarks, that Pelagius has not the idea of development. "He has not the conception of a life unfolding itself; he only recognizes the one chemical concatenation of single acts." He does not distinguish between formal and real freedom.

Augustine, on the other hand, looked upon grace as the creative principle of life, which generates as an abiding good that freedom of the will which is entirely lost in the natural man. He saw in the natural man only a liberty to do evil, since the regenerate man alone can actually will the good.

Notwithstanding the condemnation of Pelagius at the synod of Carthage (418) and of Ephesus (431), the system of Augustine did not exert much, if any, influence upon the theology of the Eastern Church.

Semipelagianism.

As Augustine held the doctrine of hereditary depravity from which no human power could deliver, and from which only the grace of God can save those who belong to the human race, he also taught that God, without any reference to the future conduct of man, has elected some out of the corrupt mass to become vessels of his mercy, and left the rest as vessels of his wrath to a just condemnation. The former act of God Augustine called predestination, the latter reprobation. He went even so far as to teach a predestination to punishment and condemnation, but not a direct predestination to sin.

But this doctrine of Augustine became to many a stone of stumbling, and there were some orthodox theologians, especially of the Greek Church, who endeavored to remove this difficulty. This prepared the way for Semipelagianism, whose advocates endeavored to pursue a middle course between the two extremes, Pelagianism and Augustinianism, by a partial adoption of the premises of both systems, without carrying them out in all their logical consequences.

The principal leaders of Semipelagianism were John Cassian, a disciple of Chrysostom, and Faustus (d. about 492), bishop of Riez in Southern Gaul. Cassian regarded the natural man neither as morally healthy (as Pelagius did), nor as morally dead (Augustine), but as diseased and morally weakened. Freedom and grace concur, sometimes the one leading, and again the other. Faustus, on the other hand, came nearer to Augustine's opinions of the doctrine of original sin than do those of Cassian, but his ideas of the nature of grace were more Pelagian than were those of Cassian.

Augustine combated Semipelagianism, but for about fifty years Semipelagianism continued to be the prevailing form of doctrine in Gaul, Augustinianism only after a variety of fortunes obtaining the preponderance in the West at the Synods of Orange and of Valence (529).

Gregory the Great (d. 604) transmitted to subsequent ages the milder aspect of the Augustinian doctrine. Along with strict Augustinianism, we find in his writings Semipelagian modifications. His views are most fully developed in his *Moralia*.

We thus see, that although Pelagianism was rejected in its

crude statements both in the East and especially in the entire Western Church, it yet really continue to influence the thinking of the Church, so that to a great extent it is true that the Roman Church praised Augustine and followed Pelagius even while it condemned him.

It was reserved for the Reformation to finish the work which Augustine left incomplete. The Lutherans developed the doctrine of faith and justification, the Calvinists, that of absolute predestination.

Scholasticism

The theologians of the Greek Church contented themselves with believing in a deterioration of the moral power of man, and laid great stress upon the freedom of the will, holding that the divine image was only obscured by the fall. John of Damascus (d. 754), the most authoritative theologian in the Eastern Church, in a certain sense may be called the "Father of Scholasticism" and the forerunner of the Scholasticism of the Middle Ages. His views were followed by the rest of the Greek theologians.

In the Western Church almost all the Schoolmen followed Augustine, though some of them adopted opinions which differed in many essential points from his fundamental principles.

In the Scholastic Theology under the influence of Anselm of Canterbury (d. 1109), the father of orthodox Scholasticism, the Augustine of the Middle Ages, this formula became predominant: "In Adam the person made the nature sinful; in his posterity, nature made the persons sinful".

According to Anselm, all self-will of the creature is an injury to the majesty of God. He expressed himself in very strict terms concerning the imputation of original sin, to the exclusion of all milder views. He however taught that only the sin of Adam is transmitted to his posterity, but not that of parents to their children, for he favored Creationism.

Peter Lombard (d. 1164) took a mediating view, holding the theory of Creationism, maintaining that original sin was wrought by sexual inclination, through which the bodily nature and with it the soul which was created and put into it, were corrupted.

Several of the later schoolmen also, especially Duns Scotus (d. 1308, at the age of 34) and his followers, manifested a leaning towards Semipelagianism, while Thomas Aquinas (d. 1274) and his school adhered more strictly to the definitions of Augustine.

Thomas Aquinas derived original sin from the unity of the organism of the race. He says, "All men who are born of Adam may be considered as one man; thus men derived from Adam are members of one body."

The essence of original sin in the Scholastic Theology was placed in the wounding of nature and the removal of grace. "Thus" says Aquinas, "original sin is, as to matter, concupiscence, as to its form, a defect or lack original righteousness." Just in proportion, however, as the relation of grace to nature was conceived of in an external manner, was the importance of original sin diminished. Sin was less and less regarded as an injury to the very being of man. Hence we find in the later theologians of the Roman Church exceeding low views of sin.

Roman Catholicism.

At the Council of Trent, in conflict with the statements of God's Word, and especially with Rom. 7: 7-8, it was declared in the fifth session that "this concupiscence which the apostle sometimes calls sin, this holy Synod declares that the Catholic Church has never under stood to be called sin, as being truly and properly sin in those born again, but because it is of sin and inclines to sin. But if any one shall think the contrary, let him be anathema."

And Bellarmine, the greatest of their old controvertialists, says, "the state of man after the fall does not differ from Adam's state in possession of pure naturals, any more than the condition of the man who has had his clothes stolen differs from the condition of a naked man. Hence the corruption of nature does not consist in the want of any natural gift, nor in the assets of any evil quality, but flows alone from the loss of the supernatural gift on account of the sin of Adam. Which decision is the common one of the scholastic doctors and of recent writers." And this is the real teaching of the Roman Catholic Church.

Lutheran Protestantism and the Augsburg Confession

Pure and original Protestantism proceeded from the profound feeling of sin and the consciousness of its guilt, and consequently was deeply interested in giving due weight to the importance of the fall and of its results.

Thus the Augsburg Confession Art. II. says:
De Peccato Originis.

1. *Item docent, quod post lapsum Adame omnes homines, secundum natu- ram propagati, nascantur cum peccato,. hoc est, sine metu Dei, sine fiducia erga Deum et cum concupiscen- tia,*

2. quodque hie morbus seu vitium originis vere sit peccatum, damnans et affe- rens nunc quoque aeternam mortem his, qui non renas- cuntur per baptismum et Spiritum Sanctum. Damnant Pelagianos et alios, qui vitium originis negant esse peccatum et, ut extenuent gloriam meriti et beneficiorum Christi, dis- putant hominem propriis viribus rationis coram Deo.

Also they teach, that since the Fall of Adam, all men begotten according to nature, are born with sin, that is, without the fear of God, without trust in God, and with concupiscence; and that this disease,. or vice of origin, is truly sin, even now condemning and bringing eternal death upon those not born again through baptism and the Holy Ghost.

They condemn the Pelagians and others, who deny that the vice of origin is sin, and who to obscure the glory of Christ's merit and benefits, argue that man can be justified before God by his own strength and reason.

Brief Outline of Or. Krauth's Lecture on Art. II. of the Augsburg Confession.

This Article of the Confession, if analyzed, will found to present either in so many words, or by just inference, the following points:

I. It affirms the unity of the Evangelical Lutheran Church in the doctrine of Original Sin.

a) A Lutheran, historically and honestly such, cannot hold

less than the Augsburg Confession, and our Church still holds the very doctrine confessed by our Fathers Augsburg.

b) If Rationalists, or Arminians, or Pelagians, or Semi Pelagians, or any others, who reject the doctrine of Original Sin, choose to call themselves Lutherans, they are willing to bear a name to which they have no just claim whatever. When a church deserts its doctrine it loses its identity.

c) A man, or body of men, may cease to be Lutheran, but a doctrine which is Lutheran once is Lutheran forever.

II. The true doctrine of sin presupposes a right Anthropology, a true doctrine of man.

1. It presupposes a sound view of man as the proper subject of redemption, capable of it and needing it.

a) Man, in his two states of integrity and corruption, touches Theology, the doctrine of God, which goes before, and Soteriology, the doctrine of the work of Christ, which follows after.

2. It presupposes a sound definition of man, as God's last and highest earthly creature, having personality, freedom, moral accountability, and immortality.

3. It presupposes that the Biblical History of man's creation is literally true; that the first pair were the immediate creation of God; and that all mankind have sprung from this one pair.

Science demonstrates that the race may have sprung from one pair inasmuch as they all belong to one species; what science shows to be possible, revelation distinctly teaches.

Science moreover exhibits the following facts:

a) As one pair is sufficient to have originated the population of the globe, the scientific presumption is strong, that there was but one pair. There is no waste of means in nature.

b) Natural science shows, that only animals of the same species produce a permanently fertile offspring, as the children of the human race.

c) The traditions of the races largely point to a common origin.

d) The languages of mankind contribute a great deal of evidence as to the original unity of the races.

e) Science does not weaken, by any of its facts, the Scripture witness to the unity of the human race.

4. It not only presupposes that the first parents of our race were the immediate creation of God, but that the Bible teaches that all their descendants are the mediate creation of God. Ps. 139:13; Acts 17:26; Heb. 12:9.

a) Of the three theories concerning the propagation of the human soul, Pre-existence, Creationism, and Traducianism, the teaching of the Lutheran Church is in favor of Traducianism, or mediate Creationism, the theory that both body, soul and spirit, are derived from the parents.

b) The true theory of Traducianism is, that it is a creation by God, of which the parents are the divinely ordained organ.

5. It presupposes, antecedent to all human sin, a state of integrity. Gen. 1:26.

a) The Confession implies that the race has fallen from a condition of glory and bliss. Man was created with an ability not to sin, which, had he been faithful, would have been matured into a condition in which he could not sin: the *posse non peccare* would have become a *non posse peccare*, and the *posse non mori* would have been merged into *non posse mori*.

6. To a correct conception of original sin it presupposes correct views of sin in general, as having its proper cause in the finite will, not in the infinite will, and! as embracing the

conaition of the finite will, as well as its overt acts.

a) God is in no respect whatever the efficient cause of sin as such, neither in part, nor in the whole; neither directly or indirectly; neither per se, nor by accident; neither in the species of Adam's fall, nor in the genus of sin of any kind. In no respect is God the cause or author of sin, or can be called such. See Ps. 5:5; Zech. 8:17; 1 John 1:5; James 1:13, 17. This sin, or want of conformity with the law, is to be ascribed to the free will of the creature, acting of its own accord. (Quenstedt.)

b) Pelagianizing Romanists contend that nothing is sin except it be voluntary. These expressions may hold good among philosophers, in judging of evil morals, but they have nothing to do with the judgment of God.

c) Scripture and sound logic teach, that to a true conception of what pertains to the will, or what is voluntary, belongs the state of the will previous to any act. Before there can be a voluntary act, there must be a state of the will which conditions that act. Original sin, therefore, is voluntary sin on this broader and more Scriptural conception of what is voluntary.

7. It presupposes that from the original state of integrity there was a fall of man into a state of sin.

a) The literal historical sense of the narrative of the Fall is the only one consistent with the obvious intent of the Holy Scriptures.

b) The serpent was but the organ of the devil.

c) The sin of the first parents embraced four distinct acts of sin; 1) incredulity, 2) affectation of the likeness of God, 3) a purpose springing from the transgression of the law, 4) a carrying out of this purpose into action. In the Fall began Original Sin.

ANTHROPOLOGY

III. The time of the operation of original sin is the whole time subsequent to the fall of Adam.

1. This implies that man was created holy. Gen. 1:26. It implies man's original holiness, the conformity of his mind to the mind of God, of his will to the will of God; in short, whatever is most completely and sharply antithetical to original sin;

2. That he lost this righteousness;

3. That with, this loss originated human sin;

4. That man's nature thereby became a sinful one.

5. It is asserted that original sin has continued in the world ever since.

a) Eve is called the mother of all living; but Adam is the source of all living, including Eve.

b) There is then but one human life in the world, the emanation of the first life, that of Adam.

c) In Adam's life and nature is the *sine qua non* of our life and nature, and Adam's sin is the *sine qua non* of our sin.

IV. The Confession teaches that the persons affected by original sin are all human beings born in the course of nature.

a) This implies that all infants, all the children our race, have original sin.

b) It implies the falseness of the Romish figment regard to the sinlessness of the mother of our Lord, therefore rejects the idea of the immaculate conception of Mary, set forth authoritatively as a doctrine of the Catholic Church by Pius IX., in 1854.

c) The Confession lays stress on the fact that original sin is by hereditary transmission, and the Formula Concord expressly rejects the idea that original sin is derived to us by imputation only.

d) That all men are embraced in the operation of original sin is clearly taught in Scripture.

1. In direct and positive assertion of the universality of original sin. Rom. 5:12, 14, 15, 18, 19.

2. In the specification of the classes embraced this universal operation of original sin. Eph. 2:3.

3. In the Scriptural negation of any limitation of universality of sin. Job 14:4.

4. In the exceptional character of Jesus Christ, alone free from original, as well as from actual sin. Cor. 5:21; Heb. 4:15; 7:26.

V. The mode of the perpetuation of original: sin is connected with the natural extension of our race.

a) The Augsburg Confession distinctly connects original sin with natural propagation and natural birth.

b) Such is the clear teaching of Scripture. Ps. 51:5; John 3:6; Eph. 2:3; Rom. 5:12.

122. VI. The great fact is asserted that all human beings are conceived in and born with sin.

a) The Scripture testimony to this great fact is very explicit. Gen. 8:21; 6:5; Ps. 14:1, 2, 3; Job 15:14; Jer. 17: 9.

b) The root of universal sinfulness must lie in the one thing common to all, man's moral condition as fallen and inheriting original sin.

VII. The results or revelations of the working of this original sin are 1) negative and 2) positive.

1. Negative:

a) Original sin shows itself first in this, that all human beings are born without the fear of God;

b) A second element is, that they are born without trust in God, without faith in Him or love for Him.

2. Positive:

a) Original sin results in this, that all human beings are born with concupiscence, that is, from their birth they are full of evil desire and evil propensity. The natural desire of an unsanctified nature is always inordinate, carnal, sensual, impure; it is desire, lust, concupiscence.

aa) The Pelagianizing Romanist says, lust, or concupiscence, brings forth sin, therefore, it cannot be sin, because the mother cannot be the child.

We reply, concupiscence brings forth sin, therefore, it must be sin, because child and mother have the same nature.

bb) Sin is in us potentially before it comes to an act.

3. As we have by nature no true fear of God, no true love of God, no true faith in God, so neither can we get them by nature.

a) In the sphere of nature, original sin leaves us in utter and hopeless ruin. 1 Cor. 2:14.

VIII. The essence of original sin involves that this disease or vice of origin is truly sin.

We affirm the doctrine of the Church:

a) Against those who deny that original sin exists.

b) Against those who deny that this defect is sin.

c) Against those who deny that original sin is and really sin.

We say concerning Original Sin

a) It is; b) It is sin; c) It is truly and really sin.

We argue that Original Sin is truly sin:

1. Because it has the relations and connections of Sin.

a) Sin is wrought in three ways:

1) when person corrupts nature, as was Adam and Eve;

2) when nature corrupts persons, as in the corruption of original sin;

3) when person corrupts person, as in actual sin, especially by example.

b) At the beginning, actual sin took the precedence and original sin followed; now, original sin takes the of cadence, and actual sin follows.

c) Original sin is begotten of sin, and hence necessity of the nature of its parent, and therefore sin.

d) It is the begetter of sin, and hence is of the nature of its child, and therefore truly sin.

e) It is the true child of true sin; the true parent of true sin, and hence is itself true sin.

2. It is truly sin, because it has the name synonyms of sin. Ps. 51:5; Rom. 5:12; John 3:6.

3. It has the essence of sin, which is deviation from the will of God.

a) Whatever is not in accordance with God's will, and this includes the condition of nature, has in it the essence of sin.

b) If the moral condition in which man is born is a deviation from the will of God, it is not depravity merely, but truly sin.

c) Not only is original sin essentially sin, but it is such pre-eminently.

d) As the nature of the potencies of a vegetable makes the vegetable world, so moral nature reveals itself in moral character.

4. We argue that original sin is truly sin because it has the attributes of sin.

Is sin evil? Gen. 6:5. Is sin unclean? Job 14: 4; 15: 14. Is sin abominable and loathsome? Job 15:15, 16. Is sin unrighteous and impure? Job 25:4. So is original sin.

5. We argue that original sin is truly sin, because it does the acts of sin.

1) It brings forth fruit unto death, Rom. 7:5.

2) The flesh serves the law of sin, Rom. 7:25.

3) The flesh lusteth against the spirit, Gal. 5:17.

4) The works of the flesh are manifest, Gal. 5:19-21.

5) The carnal mind is enmity against God, Rom. 8:7.

6) It lusteth to envy and warreth against my spiritual mind, Rom. 7:23; 6:12.

6. We argue that original sin is truly sin, because it incurs the penalties of sin. See Job 25:4, 5, 6; Rom. 7:5, 24; 8:3, 6; 5:12, 14, 15, 16, 17, 18; Rom. 8:8; Eph. 2:3.

In these passages original sin comes before us in three aspects as to penalty:

1) As punished by the penalty which comes upon the sins of act, which original sin originates.

2) As punished together with the sin of act.

3) As subject to punishment as being in itself antecedent to and separate from all sin in act

If penalty can mark its character, original sin is truly sin.

7. We argue that original sin is truly sin, because it needs the remedy of sin. Ps. 51:12; Rom. 7:24.

This remedy is needed 1) as to its essence; 2) as to its author; and 3) as to its means. Col. 2:11; John 3: 3, 5, 6; Eph. 5:25, 26.

1) The texts show who need the remedy of sin:

All human beings. As the word cannot reach an infant didactically, it must reach it sacramentally through baptism. Infants need and receive the remedy of sin. They are in common with adult believers, sanctified, and of course regenerate, washed with water, and reached by the word (Eph. 5:25, 26).

2) They show that original sin needs the essence of the remedy, the new birth, the being cleansed and sanctified.

3) They show that original sin needs the remedy of, sin as to its author, Christ who acquires it; the Holy Spirit who applies it; in general, God.

4) They show that original sin needs the remedy of sin as to its means.

a) The circumcision of Christ, that is, Holy Baptism.

b) The Word of God, didactically and sealed by the sacraments.

8. We argue, finally, that original sin is truly sin, because it is conformed to a true definition of sin.

a) Standard definition of sin in Lutheran Theology: "Sin is either a defect (want, lack, failure) or inclination, or an act conflicting with the law of God, offending God, condemned by God, and making us liable to eternal wrath and eternal punishments, had not remission been made".

b) In this definition, "the defect" and "inclination" correspond with original sin; the "act" embraces all actual sin, internal and external.

c) Or his definition he a just and true one, then original sin is truly sin.

IX. The natural consequence of this original sin is that it condemns and brings now also eternal death.

1. If original sin be truly sin, then, unchecked, it of necessity involves men in the final results of sin.

a) This is true as over against the idea that original sin brought death only to Adam, not to all his posterity.

b) Or the idea that the benefits of Christ's redemptive work need not be applied by the Holy Spirit through the appointed means.

a) Or that children, because they are born in Christendom, or of Christian parents, are on that account free from the penalty.

2. With this the language of Scripture strictly agrees. "The wages of sin is death". Rom. 6:23. See Rom. 5:12.

3. Death, even eternal death, as the endurance of suffering, is not essentially so fearful a thing as sin.

4. Original sin, if unchecked by God, brings eternal death.

5. If we have sin without an act of our will, much more may we have death, the result of that sin, without an act of our will.

6. All the visible results of Adam's sin to Adam are perpetuated to us, and this creates a powerful presumption that the invisible results of that sin are also perpetuated to us.

7. Original sin, in its own nature, is worthy of death.

Death is the wages of sin. Nature, as well as voluntary character, is regarded as properly subject to Eph. 2:3.

8. Infants are included logically, and it is also expressly taught. Rom. 5:14.

9. The results of Adam's fall and of Christ's mediation are represented as entirely parallel in the range of their subjects, the one embracing exactly the same persons as the other. Rom. 5: 15-19.

X. The natural consequence of original sin, condemnation and eternal death, is actually incurred by all who are not born again.

1. The only way that eternal death can be arrested is for its subject to he born again.

2. The relative innocence of any human being cannot in itself save him. Every man is more guilty absolutely than he is innocent relatively.

3. There is a relative innocence in the infant as contrasted with the adult, but the moral nature of the newborn infant is as truly a sinful one as that of the gray haired old reprobate, even as the physical and mental nature of the babe are as really a human nature, as that of the ripe adult. A new nature is as absolutely needed by an infant as by an adult.

4 and 5. For the same reason the relative innocence which arises from ignorance cannot save men. No man can ever reach heaven with an unchanged nature. "As many as have sinned without law shall also perish without law", Rom. 2:12.

6. Hence the testimony of Scripture is of the most explicit kind as to the absolute necessity of the new birth to every human creature. John 3:5, 6.

7. There is one absolute characteristic of all God's children, the being born of God. John 1:12, 13.

8. Before this irresistible witness of God's Word goes down the delusive idea that the work of Christ covers the case either of pagans or of infants, without their being born again.

9. Original sin must be counteracted, first, by a power which removes its penalty, and secondly, by a power which ultimately removes the sin itself.

1) The power which removes the penalty is our Lord Jesus Christ, who made atonement for original sin, as well as for the actual sins of men; this removes the *reatus* of original sin, that is, its present guilt and immediate liability.

2) The power which can remove the sin itself is in the new birth; this removes the *fomes*, the inciting fomenting power itself, or the essence of sin, which would, left to itself, ever renew the guilt and its curse.

10. The testimony of the Church through all ages is most explicit on this point, that no unregenerate human being,

infant or adult, pagan or nominal Christian, can be saved. Without holiness no man shall see the Lord,—but no man can be holy with his natural heart unchanged.

XI. When the new birth takes place, it is invariably wrought by the Holy Spirit.

XII. This new birth by the Holy Spirit has baptism as one of its ordinary means.

XIII. Baptism is the only ordinary means of universal application.
This will be denied by two classes alone:
1. By those who deny that baptism is a means of grace at all;
2. By those who deny that infants should be baptized, and who, consequently, maintain that there is no means of grace provided for them.

XIV. In maintaining the true doctrine of Original Sin, our Church, of necessity, condemns:
1. The Pelagians;
2. All others who deny that the vice of origin is
3. All who contend that man, by his own strength, can be justified before God;
4. All who thus diminish the glory of the merit of} Christ, and of His benefits.

Analysis of Article II. of the Apology on Original Sin.

This Article treats the topic under two headings,
   A. Of the notion of original sin, § 2-34;
   B. Against the adversaries of Luther, § 35-51.
   1. It restates the definition of the Augsburg Confession.

"We deny to those propagated according to carnal nature, not only the acts, but also the power or gift of producing fear and trust in God. For we say that those thus born have concupiscence, and cannot produce true fear and trust in God" . . . "When we mention concupiscence, we understand not only the acts or fruits, but the evil inclination within, which does not cease, as long as we are not born anew through the Spirit and faith". § 2, 3.

   2. Then the terms used are explained, § 4-14.
   a) Against false views it is maintained:
   1) The material of original sin is concupiscence;
   2) It is an innate, wicked desire;
   3) It is a fault or corruption in the nature of man;
   4) Not simply imputed because of Adam's sin;
   5) A personal fault or corruption;
   6) Brings eternal death;
   7) Is a vice of nature;
   8) Against all false views we call it "concupiscence", "disease", and maintain "that the nature of men is born corrupt and full of faults". § 4-6.

   6) Against the Scholastics, who extenuate the sin of origin, we assert, § 7-14;
   9) That the fear of God and faith are wanting;
   10) That the *fomes*, or evil inclination, is not simply a fault in the body, § 7;

11) Original sin is ignorance and contempt of God, the being destitute of fear and confidence in God, hatred and flight from God;

12) These diseases are in the highest degree contrary to the law of God, § 8;

13) We need the grace of Christ and the Holy Ghost to fulfill God's commandments, § 9, 10;

14) The severe diseases of original sin Scripture everywhere speaks of, Ps. 13; 14:1--3; 5:9; 140:3; 36:1; § 11;

15) The nature of men is inwardly unclean, § 12, 13. 16) For these reasons (1) we deny to man natural strength, fear and confidence in God, 2) and affirm that the faults of human nature are diseases, to-wit, ignorance of God, contempt for God, the being destitute of fear and confidence in God, and inability to love God, § 14.

3. This definition is not new, § 15-34.

1) The ancient definition expresses precisely the same thing, "Original sin is the absence of original righteousness", § 15;

(1) Righteousness comprises also the first table of the Decalogue, which teaches of the fear of God, of faith, and of the love of God, § 16;

(2) Original righteousness consisted in a more certain knowledge of God, fear of God, confidence in God, or the power to yield these affections, § 17;

(3) This is taught in Gen. 1;27, § 18;

(4) Also by Irenaeus and Ambrose, § 19;

(5) And by Paul in Eph. 5:9; Col. 3:10, § 20-22;

(6) So the ancient definition says precisely what we say, denying fear and confidence toward God, and the gifts and power to produce these acts, § 23.

2) Of the same import is the definition of Augustine:—

Original sin is concupiscence or wicked desire.

(1) Augustine includes both the defect and the vicious habit which succeeded it.

(2) Concupiscence is not only a corruption of the qualities of the body, but also in the higher powers, a vicious turning to carnal things, § 24, 25.

3) With this definition agree the wiser Scholastics.

(1) Thomas Aquinas: Original sin comprehends the loss of original righteousness, and with this an inordinate disposition of the parts of the soul; whence it is not pure loss, but a corrupt habit, § 26, 27;

(2) Bonaventura: "Original sin is immoderate concupiscence", and "the want of righteousness that is due", § 28;

(3) Hugo: Original sin is ignorance in the mind, and concupiscence in the flesh, § 29;

4) These opinions also agree with Scripture, § 30, 31;

(1) "The natural man receiveth not the things of the Spirit of God", 1 Cor. 2:14;

(2) "Sinful passions working in our members to bring forth fruit unto death", Rom. 7:5.

5) Importance of the doctrine, § 32-34.

(1) Recognition of Original Sin is necessary;

(2) The magnitude of the grace of Christ cannot be understood, unless our diseases be recognized.

(3) We must acknowledge that our heart is naturally destitute of love, fear and confidence in God.

B. Against the adversaries of Luther, § 35-51.

1. Meaning of Luther's statement that "Original Sin remains after baptism", § 35-37.

1) Baptism removes the imputation (*reatus*) of original

sin, although the material of the sin, that is, concupiscence, remains.

2) The Holy Ghost, given through baptism, begins to put to death the material, that is, concupiscence, and creates a new light, a new sense and spirit in man.

3) So Augustine: Sin is remitted in baptism, not in such a manner as that it no longer exists, but so that it is not imputed.

4) Again he says: The law which is in the members has been annulled by spiritual regeneration, and the guilt has been remitted in the sacrament, but the law remains in the mortal flesh because it occasions desires, against which believers contend.

2. Concupiscence is not merely a penalty, but is a sin subject to death and condemnation, § 38-51.

1) Luther maintains it is a sin, § 38;

2) So Paul, Rom. 7:7, 23, for he calls it a. "lust", "a law of sin which is in my members", § 39;

3) Concupiscence is sin, but it is not imputed to those who are in Christ, § 40;

4) So Augustine and the Fathers, § 41;

5) The *fomes* or evil inclination is not an adiaphoron, § 42;

6) Inner desires and thoughts are sins, even if I do not the acts or consent altogether to them, for God searches the hearts, § 43;

7) These remnants of original sin after baptism, for their non-imputation, need the grace of Christ and for their mortification, the Holy Ghost, § 44, 45;

8) Man, by his own strength, cannot fulfill the commandments of God, § 46;

9) The defects and the concupiscence are punishments and sins, § 47;

10) By our own strength we cannot free ourselves from this slavery, § 48;

11) It will not be possible to recognize the benefits of Christ until we understand our evils, § 49, 50;

12) We know that we believe aright and in harmony with the Church of Christ, § 51.

18, Analysis of Article on Sin in Smalcald Articles.

1. True doctrine, § 1-3.

1) Sin originated and entered into the world from one man, Adam, by whose disobedience all men were made sinners, and subject to death and the devil. Rom. 5:12, 19.

2) The fruits of this original sin are afterwards evil deeds.

3) This hereditary sin is so deep and horrible a corruption of nature, that no reason can understand it, but it must be learned and believed from Scripture, Ps. 51:5; Rom. 5:12, 13, 14; Ex. 33:3; Gen. 3:7 ff.

147. 2. False doctrine of the Scholastics, § 4-11.

1) That since the fall of Adam the natural powers of man have remained entire and incorrupt;

2) That man has a free will to do good and omit evil;

3) That man by his natural powers can observe and do all the commands of God;

4) That by his natural powers he can love God above all things, and his neighbor as himself;

5) That if a man do what he can, God certainly grants to him his grace;

6) That for a good work, the Holy Ghost with his grace is not necessary.

Conclusion.

1) If these false doctrines would be right, Christ has died

in vain, since there is in man no sin or misery for which He should have died.

Analysis of Article on Original Sin, in Epitome, Formula of Concord.

1. Statement of the controversy, § 1.

   1) Is there, since the fall, a distinction between man's nature, or essence, and Original Sin, so that nature is one thing, and Original Sin, which inheres in the corrupt nature and corrupts the nature, is another?

2. Affirmative statement of the pure doctrine.

   1) We believe, teach and confess that there is a distinction between the nature itself, which ever since the fall is and remains a creature of God, and Original Sin, and that this distinction is as great as a distinction between a work of God and a work of the devil, § 2;

   2) The reasons for this distinction, § 3-7;

   (1) If no distinction is made between our corrupt human nature and original sin, it conflicts with the chief articles of Christian faith, concerning Creation, Redemption, Sanctification, and the Resurrection of the body, § 3;

   (2) For God mediately creates our bodies and since the fall, notwithstanding that they are corrupt, and they are His work, Job 10:8; Deut. 32:18: Isa. 45:9, 10; 54:5; 64:8; Acts 17:28; Ps. 100:3; 139:14; Eccles. 12:1, § 4;

   (3) True human nature, "yet without sin", the Son of God has assumed into the unity of his person, Heb. 2:14, 16; 4:15, § 5;

   (4) This human nature Christ has redeemed, sanctified, raises from the dead and gloriously adorns as his, work , but Original

Sin he has not created, assumed, sanctified; he also will not raise it, § 6, 7.

3) The extent of Original Sin, § 810.

(1) This original sin is not a slight, but so deep a corruption of human nature, that nothing healthy remains, § 8;

(2) This unspeakable injury cannot be discerned by the reason, but only from God's word, § 9;

(3) No one but God can separate nature from this corruption of nature, and yet this fully comes to pass at death, § 10.

3. Negative statement of the rejection of false doctrines, § 1125.

1) Pelagian errors, § 11 14.

(1) We reject the doctrine that original sin is only a *reatus* or debt, on account of what has been committed by another and so imputed to us, but maintain that it is a real corruption of our nature, § 11;

(2) We reject the error that evil lusts are not true sin, and maintain that man remains a child of wrath, until engrafted into Christ, § 12.

(3) We reject the error that man's nature, ever since the fall, is incorrupt, and that with respect to spiritual things, it has remained entirely good and pure, § 13;

(4) We reject the error that original sin is only external, a slight stain dashed upon nature, § 14.

2) Synergistic errors, § 15, 16.

(1) We reject the error that it is only an external impediment to unimpaired spiritual powers, and that this stain can be easily washed away as pigment from the wall, § 15;

(2) Also, that in man human nature and essence are not entirely corrupt, and that man still has ability in spiritual things to begin to work, or to co-work for something good, § 16.

3) Manichaean errors, § 17-19.

(1) We reject the false dogma that original sin has been infused into the nature of man, and intermingled with it, as poison and wine are mixed, § 17;

(2) Also that not the natural man, not the nature, but only original sin in the nature, is accused, § 18;

(3) Also that original sin is the nature and essence itself of the corrupt man, so that we cannot conceive of a distinction between the corrupt nature, considered by itself, and Original Sin, § 19.

4) Other distinctions made, § 20-25.

(1) Luther calls Original Sin natural sin, personal and essential sin, that by such words he might indicate the distinction between Original Sin which inheres in human nature, and actual sins, § 20;

(2) Original Sin inheres in the nature and essence of man, is born in us, and is the fountain-head of all actual sins, as wicked thoughts, words and works, Matt. 15:19; Gen. 6:5; 8:21, § 21;

(3) Nature may mean the very substance of man, when we say, God created human nature,—or it mean the vicious quality of a thing, which inheres in nature or essence, as when we say, the nature and disposition of man is to sin, and is sin. By nature we do not mean the substance of man, but something that inheres:" in the substance, § 22;

(4) In human nature we must distinguish between the essence, and Original Sin which is attached to it in an accidental way, § 23, 24;

(5) Original sin is the work of the devil, and he only, in an accidental way, God permitting, corrupt substance created by God, § 25.

20. Analysis of Article on Original Sin in Solid Declaration

Formula of Concord.

1. Statement of the controversy, § 1-3.

1) Some hold that now since the fall, because the nature is corrupt through sin, there is no distinction whatever between the nature and essence of man and original sin, § 1;

2) Others maintain that a distinction must be observed between the nature and essence of the corrupt man, i. e., his body or soul, which as the creatures of God pertain to us even since the fall, and Original Sin, which is a work of the devil, whereby the nature has become corrupt, § 2;

3) If this doctrine be rightly presented from and according to God's Word, and be separated from all errors, the benefits of Christ and his precious merit, and the gracious efficacy of the Holy Ghost, will be better known and the more extolled, § 3.

2. The pure Scriptural doctrine, § 4-15.

1) We should recognize as sins not only actual sins, but also the horrible, dreadful, hereditary malady whereby the entire nature is corrupted,—and this original sin should be recognized as the chief sin, which is the root and fountainhead of all actual sins, and as a spiritual leprosy by which man is thoroughly and utterly infected and corrupted before God, § 4-6;

2) God is not the creator, author or cause of sin, but from the instigation of the devil, through one man, sin, which is the

work of the devil, has entered the world (Rom. 5:12; 1 John 3:7), and Original Sin is propagated from sinful seed, through carnal conception and birth, §7;

3) What and how great this hereditary evil is, no reason knows and understands, but it must be learned from Scripture, § 8;

(1) This hereditary evil is the cause of our all being in God's displeasure, and by nature children of wrath (Rom. 5:12-14; Eph. 2:3), § 9;

(2) There is an entire want of concreated original righteousness, and likewise an inability and unfitness for all the things of God, for there is no power for beginning and effecting anything in spiritual things, § 10;

(3) Man, since the fall, also receives by inheritance an inborn wicked disposition, an inward impurity of heart, wicked lusts and propensities, § 11, 12.

4) The punishment of Original Sin, § 13.

1) The penalties are death, eternal damnation, and also other bodily and spiritual, temporal and eternal miseries;

2) The tyranny and dominion of the devil, who stupefies and leads astray many great and learned men into heresy and other blindness, and delivers men to all sorts of crime.

5) The remedy for Original Sin, § 14, 15.

(1) It can be covered and forgiven before God only for Christ's sake, and in the baptized and believing;

(2) It can be healed only by the regeneration and renewal of the Holy Ghost, begun in this life, and fully completed at death.

3. False doctrines that are rejected, § 16-49.

1) Pelagian errors, § 17-25.

(1) That original sin is only a *reatus* or debt, without any corruption of our nature, § 17;

(2) That evil lusts are not sins, § 18;

(3) That they are not properly and truly sin, § 19;

(4) That nature, ever since the fall, is incorrupt, with respect to spiritual things entirely good and pure, § 20;

(5) That original sin is only external, a slight insignificant stain dashed upon the nature of man, but this nature retains its integrity and power even in spiritual things, § 21;

(6) That it is not a deficiency, but only an external impediment to our spiritual good powers, as when a magnet is smeared with garlic-juice, § 22;

(7) That our nature has not entirely lost all with respect to divine things, but has the capacity, or aptness in spiritual things to begin to work or co-work something, § 23;

(8) All these doctrines are rejected, because Word teaches that the corrupt nature, of and by itself, can do nothing but sin, Gen. 6:5; 8:21; § 25.

159. 2) Manichaean errors rejected, § 26-49.

(1) That though in the beginning human nature created by God pure and good, afterwards Original Sin from without is infused and mingled by Satan, as something essential, in the nature, as poison is mingled with wine, § 26;

(2) Satan has not created or made something essentially evil, and mingled it with man's nature, § 27;

(3) Original Sin is not something existing of itself in or apart from the nature of corrupt man, nor is it the peculiar essence of the corrupt man, or the man himself, § 28;

(4) We cannot distinguish between the corrupt nature of man and original sin, as though the nature before God were pure, good and holy, but the original sin alone which dwells therein were evil, § 29;

(5) No; God does not only accuse and condemn the original sin in human nature, but the entire nature as corrupt by sin, § 30;

(6) As in external leprosy the body which is leprous, and the leprosy in the body, are not properly speaking one thing, so the corrupt nature in which dwells the Original Sin which corrupts the entire man, differs, and we must consider it as distinct, from Original Sin which dwells in man's nature, § 31-33.

(7) We are compelled to preserve this distinction between corrupted human nature and original sin, by the articles 1) of Creation, 2) of Redemption, 3) of Sanctification, 4) of Resurrection, § 34-49.

1. Arguments from the Article of Creation, § 35-42.

1) Since the fall man is a creature and work of God, Job 10:8-12; Ps. 139:14-16; Deut. 32:6; Isa. 45:11; 54:5; 64:8; Eccl. 12:7; Acts 17:25; Rev. 4:16, § 37;

2) Therefore the corrupt man cannot be, without any distinction, sin itself, for otherwise God would be a Creator of sins, § 38;

3) In His unspeakable goodness God through mercy cleanses this corrupt, perverted human nature all sin, sanctifies and saves it; § 39;

4) Original Sin then does not originate with God, is not a

creature or work of God, but a work of the devil, § 40;

5) We conclude, then, that the nature is corrupted, that thoughts, words and works of corrupt nature are wicked, is originally the work of Satan, who, through sin, corrupted God's work in Adam, and this Original Sin is transmitted by inheritance to us, § 41, 42. ·

2. Arguments for this distinction from the Article of Redemption, § 43, 44.

1) The Son of God assumed our human nature, yet without sin, Heb. 2:14;

2) Inasmuch as the Son of God assumed our nature, and not original sin, it is clear that human nature and original sin are not one thing, but must be distinguished.

3. Argument from Article of Sanctification, § 45.

1) God cleanses, washes and sanctifies men from sin (1 John 1:7) and Christ saves his people from their sins (Matt. 1:21). Sin, therefore, cannot be man himself; for God, for Christ's sake, receives man into grace, but He remains hostile to sin to eternity.

164. 4. Arguments from Article of Resurrection, § 46, 47.

1) Our body shall arise, but without sin;

2) If there were no difference, Original Sin would also arise, and remain in eternal life in the elect.

(8) We reject, therefore, this doctrine of the Manichaeans that Original Sin is the substance or nature of corrupt man,

and that there is no distinction between our corrupt nature and Original Sin, § 48, 49.

4. Explanation of terms used, § 50-62.

1) "Nature", § 50-53.
   (1) It is best to use and retain the same words, § 50;
   (2) Not to use words in several senses, § 51;
   (3) Original sin properly signifies the deep corruption of our nature, § 52;
   (4) "Natural sin", "personal sin", "essential sin", mean that the entire nature, person and essence of man is entirely corrupted by Original Sin, § 53.

2) "Substance" and "accident", § 54-62.
   (1) Among learned men everything is either "substance", an independent essence, or "accident", an incidental matter which does not exist by itself essentially, but exists in another independent essence, and can be distinguished therefrom, § 54;
   (2) Every self-existing essence, as far as it is a substance, is either God Himself, or a work and creation of God. Hence, with Augustine we say, Original Sin is not man's nature or substance itself, but is an incidental defect and damage in the nature, an accident, something incidental, § 55, 56;
   (3) Original Sin is no substance, but an accident, § 57;
   (4) Ministers of the Church must not remain in doubt as to whether Original Sin be a substance or accident, § 58;
   (5) Scriptures testify that this Original Sin is an unspeakable evil, such an entire corruption of human nature that in it and all its internal and external powers nothing pure or good remains,

and that man is in God's sight truly and spiritually dead, § 60;

(6) When we say Original Sin is an accident we not extenuate Original Sin, § 61;

(7) But with Luther we say, "We are infected by the poison of Original Sin from the sole of the foot to the crown of the head, inasmuch as this happened to us in a nature still perfect", § 62.

Presentation of the Doctrine of Original Sin by our Dogmaticians.

1. Distinction between original sin originating and originated.

1) Quenstedt: Originating original sin is that vicious act which our first parents committed, which act has not passed over to their posterity, nor is found in them except by imputation only. However, this sin gave origin to the deep corruption of man, which is called passive or originated original sin, which is a vicious habit, contracted by Adam through that actual transgression of the divine law, and propagated to his posterity.

2. The reason why called original sin.

1) Because derived from Adam, the root and beginning of the human race;

2) Because it is connected with the origin of the descendants of Adam;

3) Because it is the origin and fountain of actual transgressions (Hollaz).

169. 3. Definition of Original Sin.

1) Hollaz: Original sin is (1) a want of original righteousness, (2) connected with a depraved inclination, (3) corrupting in the most inward parts the whole human nature, (4) derived from the fall of our first parents, (5) and propagated to all men by

natural generation, (6) rendering them indisposed to spiritual good, but inclined to evil, (7) and making them the objects of divine wrath and eternal condemnation.

How this connate depravity is called in Scripture.

1) Indwelling sin, Rom. 7:17;
   2) Besetting sin, Heb. 12:1;
   3) A law in the members, Rom. 7:23;
   4) An evil lying near, Rom. 7:21.

Scriptural proofs of the existence of Original Sin.

Important passages are Gen. 6:5; 8:21; Job 14:4; 15:14; Ps. 14:2, 3; 51:5; 58:3; John 3: 5,6; Eph. 2:3. Especially Ps. 51:5; Gen. 5:3; Rom. 5:12-14.

172. 6. Chemnitz on Rom. 5:12-14.

1) The efficient cause of Original Sin is shown to be the first man;

2) The subjects affected by Original Sin are all men who come into the world;

3) The punishment is not only the death of the body; but the reign of death and the sentence of condemnation,

4) Paul affirms that the whole world is guilty, both in consequence of the one sin of the first man, and because all have been constituted sinners;

5) He indicates that even they have original sin who have not sinned alter the similitude of Adam's transgression;

6) He describes the manner in which original sin is propagated,—by one man.

The form of Original Sin.

1) It is a depravity negative, the lack of original righteousness, being without the good which should exist, so that men are by nature children of wrath, Eph. 2:1, 3; Ps. 14:3; Rom. 3:10-12, 23;

2) It is a depravity positive, the most complete corruption of the whole nature, desirous of the evil which should not exist,—even a wickedness, lust or concupiscence, directly opposite to original righteousness, Rom 7: 17, 20, 21; Heb. 12: 1. (Quenstedt.)

The particular parts of Original Sin.

1) In respect of the intellect, a) a total want of spiritual light, and b) a proneness to form rash and false judgments concerning spiritual things;

2) In respect of the will, want of ability a) to love God above all things, b) to perform what the intellect has dictated aright, c) to restrain the appetites in a proper manner, and d) on the contrary, the will is inclined to sinful acts;

3) In respect to the sensuous appetite there is a) a want of obedience to the higher faculties, b) a rushing into things agreeable to the senses though prohibited by the divine law, c) not waiting for, or rejecting, the decision of reason. (Baier.)

The consequences of Original Sin.

1) It is not only the foundation and fountain of all actual sin, but also has, as its consequence, the wrath of God and temporal and eternal punishment;

2) As it inheres in the sinner as a shameful stain, the sinner is regarded detestable, and the consequence of this sin is that he is held responsible for guilt (*reatus culpae*) and liable to punishment (*reatus poenae*), unless by faith he obtains forgiveness of actual sins, and so also of original sin.

Though our dogmaticians lay stress on hereditary transmission of Original Sin by natural propagation, they do not deny that Adam's sin is also imputed to his posterity.

1) By natural propagation. Hollaz: Everything follows the seeds of its own nature. No black crow ever produces a white dove, nor a ferocious lion a gentle lamb; and no man polluted with inborn sin ever begets a holy child;

2) By imputation. Hollaz: The first sin of Adam, since he is regarded as the common parent, head, root, and representative of the whole race, is truly and justly imputed by God, for guilt and punishment, to all his posterity.

3) Quenstedt on Rom. 5:12, says: It makes little difference whether we translate "in whom all sinned" or "in that all sinned" for in either case Adam's sin is imputed to all.

(1) "In whom", that is, in Adam, who represented the persons of all his prosperity, all sinned, for our first parents were then considered not only as the first individuals of the human race, but also the true root, stock, the natural and also the moral source of the whole human race. Hence we are said to have been in the loins of our first parents. And thus God imputes most justly to his posterity the sin of Adam unto

condemnation.

(2) "In that" (or "because" or "inasmuch as"), that is, all die because they have sinned. Therefore infants die because they have sinned. But infants and those not yet born, die either on account of some fault of their own or of an actual transgression; therefore, it is on account of the actual transgression of another, of Adam, who tainted them with his own stain.

4) Quenstedt distinguishes between immediate and mediate imputation.

(1) The first Adamitic sin is immediately imputed to us so far as we existed already in Adam.

(2) The sin of Adam is mediately imputed to us so far as original sin is mediately inherent in our own persons and individually, contaminated from that same Adam.

The adjuncts of Original Sin.

1) Natural inherence, Heb. 12:1; Rom. 7:21. It is therefore, not a substance, but an accident.

2) Natural transmissibility, Gen. 5:3; Job 14:4; Ps. 51:5; John 3:6; Eph. 2:3.

3) Duration, or obstinate inherence during life, Rom. 7:17; Heb. 12:1.

ANTHROPOLOGY

Four things are worthy of attention in considering the duration of Original Sin.

(1) The inflammable material habitually inhering, or the root, which is removed in the dissolution of the soul and body;

(2) The sense of this root, which is removed in death;

(3) The dominion of it, which is gradually and successfully overcome, but not completely here, in sanctification;

(4) The guilt of it, removed in regeneration and justification.

Signification of expression "Original sin is inherent in our nature".

1) "Original sin is not the very substance of man . . . but that which inheres in it alter the manner of an accident; for it is distinguished in the Scriptures, Rom. 7:20, from the essence itself of man, and is called indwelling sin; now, as an inhabitant or guest is not the same as the house, so neither is sin the same as man";

2) It is not a mere accident, lightly and externally attached, but internally and intimately inhering, and therefore called, the easily besetting sin (Heb. 12:1);

3) It is an accident connate and natural, produced together with, and in the nature, so that it is not any temporary and transient accident, but is fixed and permanent. Quenstedt.

The Virgin Mary is not excepted from Original Sin. Our dogmaticians reject the idea of the immaculate conception of the Virgin Mary, that is, that she was conceived and born without sin, a doctrine that had been maintained by the Franciscans, Scotists and Jesuits, but denied by the Thomists and Dominicans, but was finally authoritatively set forth on Dec. 8, 1854, by Pius IX, as a doctrine of the Roman Catholic Church. Since the twelfth century it has been almost the universal idea that the Virgin Mary was preserved from actual sin, but the Roman Catholic Church now teaches that she had been wholly exempt from all sin, original and actual, throughout her life and in her death.

§ 3. Modern Criticism.

The View of the Socinians and the Older Unitarians.

1) We here speak of the more sober and conservative older Unitarians. Modern Unitarianism in the United States has followed essentially the same development as in England, and passed through the stages of Arminianism, Arianism, Antitritheism, to rationalism and a modernism based on a large-minded acceptance of the results of the comparative study of all religions. Unitarian thought in the United States has passed through three periods. The first, from 1800 to 1835, was formative, mainly influenced by English philosophy, and was semi-supernaturalistic, and imperfectly rationalistic. The second period, from 1835 to 1885, profoundly influenced by German idealism, was increasingly rationalistic, while its third period, beginning about 1885, has been one of rationalism, recognition of universal religion, and a large acceptance of the scientific method and ideas.[31]

---

[31] See COOKE, Article on Unitarianism, Encyclopedia Britannica. 11th edition.

2) The older Unitarians teach that through sin Adam and his descendants have not lost free choice. In so far as original sin is the denial of this freedom, Socinianisrn disputes it emphatically. They hold that original sin as depravity of the choice of the good and as a penalty impending over man contradicts Scripture. Lust and inclination to sin, in which original sin is said to consist, are possible in all but not shown to be in all. If there were such lust, that it is the result of Adam's sin would not follow. If it were, original sin would cease to be sin. Hence there is no original sin as such. After the fall, man, mortal by nature, was abandoned to his natural mortality because of the sin of Adam. There is produced a certain sinful disposition by the continuous sinning of all generations. Accordingly, the freedom of man is weakened, but with the aid of God man may appropriate salvation.[32]

Arminianism and its Modern Representative, Methodism.

1) Arminianism maintains that in order to true responsibility, guilt, penalty, especially eternal penalty, there must be in the agent a free-will, and this freedom of the will must consist in the power, even in the same circumstances and under the same motives, of choosing either way, good or evil.

None but the person who freely commits the sin can be guilty of that sin. One person cannot be guilty of another's sin. There can be no vicarious guilt, and so literally and strictly there can be no vicarious punishment.

The race inherits the nature of fallen Adam, not by being

---

[32] See ZOECKLER, Article on Socinus, New Schaff-Herzog Encyclopedia.

held guilty of his sin, but by the law of natural descent, just as all posterity inherit the physical, mental, and moral qualities of the progenitor.

Arminianism, denying that the race is judicially guilty for Adam's sin, affirms the salvation of all infants. Man is born in a "state of initial salvation", and the means of final salvation are amply placed within the reach of his free choice.

It maintains that there are doubtless many in pagan lands saved even by the, to them, unknown Redeemer.[33]

The system of Arminius was more fully expounded by Limborch and Episcopius. Many so-called Arminians, as Whitboy and others, were rather Pelagians. John Wesley greatly modified and improved the Arminian doctrine.

Wesleyanism holds that the guilt of all through Adam was removed by the justification of all through Christ, and that man has the ability to co-operate with God, by the aid of the Holy Spirit through the universal influence of the redemption of Christ. Wesleyanism was systematized by Watson and his form of Wesleyanism is nearer to Scripture than Arminianism proper. Pope, in his Theology, follows more closely Wesley and Watson, but Whedon and Raymond in America, represent more fully original Arminianism.

But all such views are unscriptural.

1) The offer of universal grace does not remove man's depravity or his condemnation, unless this grace is applied and not rejected, as is evident from a proper interpretation of Rom. 5:12-19; Eph. 2:3;

2) We can see how little the Methodists mean by " "sin" from

---

[33] See WHEDON, Article on Arminianism, Johnson's Universal Cyclopaedia.

the statement of Sheldon, one of their dogmaticians, that "guilt cannot possibly be a matter of inheritance, and consequently original sin can be affirmed of the posterity of Adam only in the sense of hereditary corruption, which first becomes an occasion of guilt when it is embraced by the will of the individual";

3) No sin without consent, therefore no guilt in evil desire. This is the same as the Romanist doctrine concupiscence;

4) According to this view the law condemns only volitional transgression, and man has no organic moral connection with the race.

The Federal Theory, or Theory of the Covenants.

The Federal Theory had its origin with Cocceius (1603-1669), professor at Leyden, but was more fully elaborated by Turretin (1623-1687). This has become a tenet of the Reformed as distinguished from the Lutheran Church, and its main advocates have been the Princeton school of theologians, of whom Charles Hodge was the great representative. George Fisher in his Discussians gives us a very clear account of the Federal Theory and its origin. 1) The covenant is a sovereign constitution imposed by God; 2) Federal union is the legal ground of imputation; 3) Our guilt for Adam's sin is simply a legal responsibility; 4) That imputed sin is punished by inborn depravity, and that inborn depravity by eternal death. According to this theory God immediately creates each soul of Adam's posterity with a corrupt and depraved nature, which infallibly leads to sin, and which is itself sin. This is the theory of the immediate imputation of Adam's sin to his posterity, their corruption of nature, being the effect and not the cause of that imputation.

1) But there is no mention of such a covenant with Adam in Scripture;

2) And Scripture declares that through Adam's sin were made sinners (Rom. 5:19), not simply regarded treated as sinners;

3) It implies the doctrine of immediate Creationism, is entirely contrary to Scripture and makes God the author of sin;

4) This theory regards the soul as originally pure until imputation. The Federal theory "makes sin in us the penalty of another's sin, instead of being the penalty of our own sin, as on the Augustinian scheme, which regards depravity in us as the punishment of our own sin in Adam."

Rationalism.

Rationalism has made it a reproach that the doctrine of original sin lies at the foundation of the evangelical system.

5

The Essential Character of Sin

Divisions.

1) Sin does not originate from the sensuous or finite nature of man, 2) but in his free will, 3) which perverts itself to self-seeking, in disobedience towards God, 4) thereby has brought man into guilt and punishment.

The subject naturally divides itself into the doctrine of Scripture and the Church doctrine.

§ 1. The Doctrine of Scripture.

The Formal Principle of Sin.

1) From the biblical account of the fall in Gen 3 we learn that man can pass from the state of innocence into the possession of moral character only by an act of self-determination.

2) He had to distinguish his will from the good itself, hence the good is placed before him objectively, in the form of a command, Gen. 2:16, 17. If the will is objectively confronted by what is good, and it thereupon distinguishes itself from the good, still this does not involve a decision of the will against the good.

3) The will of man does not immediately react against the divine command, but Scripture refers the first impulse to a decision against the command to an operation of an influence from without, and represents the woman (Gen. 3:1-3) as at first still acknowledging the obligatory force of the divine command.

4) When the woman (3:2, 3) remembers the divine command, and knows that she is bound by it, and thus acknowledges its obligatory force, she has not yet sinned, and she knows that she has a conscience.

5) Hence it follows, that, according to the Old Testament, sin is not a necessary factor in the development of man, but a product of free choice.

6) The chief thing in this connection is that the seduction does not at all act by compulsion on many but is successful only when man voluntarily ceases to resist temptation.

The Material Principle of Sin.

The following is the process of the origin of sin:

(1) Doubt is awakened as to whether what God has commanded is really good, Gen. 3:1; and then v. 4 proceeds to a decided denial of God's word;

(2) Then selfishness, a rebelling against God's will and God's

word, is awakened;

(3) Then sensuous allurement exerts its power, Gen. 3:6.

The real principle of sin, therefore, according to the Old Testament, is, (1) unbelief of the divine word; (2) the selfish elevation of self-will above the divine will; and (3) the presumptuous trampling upon the limits set by divine command.

The real principle of evil does not lie in matter, in the body. It is a fundamental doctrine of the Old Testament that evil is originally the denial of the divine will,—that sin is sin because man selfishly exalts himself above God and His will.

We are not to think of God as an envious being, but as the Holy one, and holiness cannot bear anything contradictory to itself. It is preposterous to take the words of Gen. 3:22, "The man is become as one of us" as an expression of divine envy,—it rather contains a mournful irony, for man by the Fall had really reached what he was to reach, but in a wrong way, and to his hurt. He had reached independence over against God; but Satan had deceived and deluded him, for it was independence in evil only. Instead of being raised to free communion with God, he is free to go upon ungodly paths.

Whether the account of the fall of Adam is referred to in the later books of the Old Testament cannot be affirmed with entire certainty. Most probably such passages as Hos. 6:7; Job 31:33, refer to the Fall, and are correctly translated in the text of the Revised Version. The passage in Isa. 43:27, "the first father sinned" refers evidently to Abraham, for Adam is not the ancestor of Israel, but rather of humanity.

The Old Testament designations for sin.

These names for sin are to be understood in conformity with the account we have given of the principle of sin. They relate rather to the form or manifestation of; sin than to its essence, and their full force is only to be reached by the antithesis in which they stand.

1) The most common expression is *chattath* (and its allied forms, occurring first in Gen. 4:7), translated in the Septuagint *hamartia*, having the force "wandering from the way", denoting a missing, or deviation from the divine way and the goal prescribed for man by the divine will. It comprehends sins of weakness as well as sins of wickedness.

2) The second expression, *Avon*, means properly crookedness, perversion, and primarily designates· the character of an action. It is the perversion of the divine law, *anomia*; then especially the guilt of sin, first in Gen. 15: 16, and so in many connections.

3) In all its intensification, sin becomes *pesha*, apostasy, rebellion against God. While *chattath* includes sins of negligence and weakness, design and set purpose are always implied in pesha. The chief passage is Job 34:37, "He addeth rebellion unto his sin".

According to Delitzsch on Ps. 32:1, "Sin is called *pesha*, as being a breaking loose from God, breach of faith, fall from the state of grace; *chattath* as being a missing of the divinely appointed goal, a deviation from what is pleasing to God; *avon* as a perversion, distortion, misdeed". Hitzig says these three terms combined "exhaust the idea of sin".

4) If the evil has become an habitual feature of the disposition and of the actions, it is *Resha*, godlessness, wickedness. The

underlying idea is, to be under stormy excitement, to be turbulent, fractious.

5) Evil, as in itself empty and worthless, is called *'Aven*. It includes the idea of nothingness, and more remotely involves the idea of exhaustion.

6) The idea couched in many of the Old Testament phrases is that sin is impotence, the weakness of moral nature, moral impotence.

7) Many of these terms consider life as a journey or course, holiness as the true path or as running on that course, and sin as the wandering or flying from the path, or lingering idly in it. The fellowship of God is the something which all these images suppose to be lost through sin.

The New Testament names for sin.

A mournful catalog of words based on a great variety of images, is used in the New Testament to describe the taint of sinfulness which man inherits from his birth and which marks his moral character and actions.

1) Sometimes it is set forth as the missing of aim or mark, *hamartia*, very common in the Septuagint as translation of *chattath*. This word denotes missing the goal conformable to and fixed by God, because human action misses its destination, and there with the will of God. It denotes not so much sin considered as an action, as sin considered as the quality of an action; that is, sin generically Original sin is *hamartia*, the missing of perfection, the defect of our nature.

2) Sometimes it is set forth as a transgressing of a line, *parabasis*, crossing a forbidden way. This designates sin as

deviation from the prescription of the law, and thus denotes sin, as far as it is imputed, as a violation of the law. The word occurs seven times in the New Testament, always in the writings of Paul (twice in Hebrews). Actual sin alone is *parabasis*, and involve us in personal guilt.

3) Sometimes it is regarded as disobedience to a voice, *parakoe*, taking no heed, disobeying, translated disobedience. It denotes rebellious conduct towards the revealed will of God.

4) Sometimes it is designated as a fall or false step, *paraptoma*, denoting a missing or falling short of a divine command, a missing and violation of right. It is a word not quite as strong as *parabasis*, which denotes sin objectively viewed, as a violation of a known rule of life, while in *paraptoma* reference is made especially to the subjective passivity and suffer fog of him who misses and falls short of the enjoined command. The word has come to be used of great and serious guilt, and generally of all sin, even though unknown and unintentional (Gal. 6:1).

5) Once it is set forth as a mistake or as ignorance of what ought to have been done, as *agnoema* (Heb. 9:7), denoting not only unconscious sin, but generally all sin which may enter into consciousness, but which does not proceed from consciousness.

6) Again it is regarded as discomfiture, defeat, loss, as *hettema*, and in 1 Cor. 6:7 as defect, loss as respects salvation, Thus also in Rom. 11:12.

7) Twice it is regarded as a debt, *opheilema*, Matt. 6:12; Rom. 4:4; that which one owes or is bound to. This denotes sin as dereliction of duty, not so much the duty omitted as the duty still to be rendered,—that is, by satisfaction. Sin, accordingly, is *opheilema*, because it imposes on the sinner the necessity of making atonement, of rendering satisfaction, or of undergoing

punishment.

8) Sometimes it is set forth absolutely as *anomia*, disobedience to law, lawlessness. The last figure is employed in the most general definition of sin given in the New Testament, sin is lawlessness, 1 John 3:4. It denotes sin in its relation to God's will and law; that which, like *parabasis*, makes it guilt, Rom. 7:13. Sin can be imputed because it is *anomia*. The law of God is the rule of the actions of men, and whatsoever is done by man, or is in man, having any contrariety or opposition to the law of God, is sin.

9) But the special Biblical designation of sin is flesh, *sarx*. Even in the Old Testament the word flesh has an ethical signification, as in Gen. 6:3. Ordinarily in the Old Testament it designates human nature as fallen and subject to death. In the New Testament it occurs almost always in the ethical sense.

The sense of *sarx* as flesh in the New Testament may be reduced to the following heads:

(1) The earthly, material substance of man. 1 Cor. 15:39, "there is one flesh of man, and another flesh of beasts"; Eph. 5:29, "No man ever hateth his own flesh".

(2) Man as far as he, according to his fleshly being, is like other earthly creatures. 1 Pet. 1:24, "all flesh is: as grass"; Ps. 65:2.

(3) The sensuous, phenomenal nature of man in general, including his mind, consequently not the body: in antithesis to the spirit, but man in antithesis to God. John 1:14, "The Word became flesh, and dwelt among us". This verse states that the Word of God assumed a human nature, composed of body, soul and spirit, where flesh, though it be a name drawn from the visible part of man, includes the spirit also. The biblical view of the personality of man involves so strict a unity of body

and soul that it does not hesitate to transfer the terms which belong to man as body to his soul, or those belonging to man as spiritual to his body;—"My flesh crieth out unto the living God", Ps. 84:2; "My soul cleaveth unto the dust", Ps. 119:25.

(4) It designates man as through his nature he be· longs to the world and stands in fellowship with it, so that under the term flesh, the entire compass of the natural life, including the individual thinking, is subsumed. As in Matt. 16:17, "Flesh and blood hath not revealed it unto thee, but my Father which is in heaven"; as also Rom. 11:14, "Them that are my flesh".

(5) It designates man as standing in fellowship with the world in his present natural state, on the side of the mortality of his nature, as also on the side of his sinfulness. So already in the Old Testament, Isa. 40:6; Ps. 78:39; but especially so in the New Testament, as in John 3:6, in opposition to the Holy Spirit, "that which is born of the flesh is flesh"; Rom. 7:18. This involves not simply the sensuous, but also the purely intellectual aspect of man, as in 2 Cor: 10:25; Gal. 3:3; 5:19-21; Col. 2:18.

10) As constituent elements of sin, prominence is given to its aspect (1) as *epithumia*, lust, Rom. 7:7; Gal. 5:16; James 1:14, 15; (2) as seeking his own, 1 Cor. 10:24; Phil. 2:4, 21; (3) as enmity against God, Rom. 8:7; James 4:4.

11) The consequences of sin are guilt and death. Rom. 3:19, "under the judgment of God". This guilt brings upon men the wrath of God (Eph. 2:3), which ends in death.

Summary of the Scripture Doctrine of Sin.

According to the testimony of Scripture, in the words of an able conservative Biblical scholar,[34] Sin is not:

(1) The result of the opposition of two eternally antagonistic principles, one good and the other evil; nor

(2) The consequence of the fruitless action of a beneficent Being on an intractable material, eternal as Himself, limiting Him, and thwarting His power; nor

(3) An essential part of the nature of man;

but Sin is:

(4) The result of a subtle tempter's power operating upon and deceiving the parent of the race;

(5) A perverse assertion of independence on the part of man in his relation to God;

(6) An abuse of free-will; a choosing to please self rather than to please God;

(7) At the root it is selfishness. The inmost nature of sin, the determining principle which runs through it in all its forms, is selfishness.

Sin is not a substance or a thing. There is nothing in itself evil. All things that are, are God's creation, and good. Evil is simply the disorder introduced into things by the perversity of the creature in abusing his free-will, and asserting-what is the essence of all sin—independence of God.

4) Sin is the fault and corruption of man's nature. Its seat and source is in the will.

---

[34] Compare MACLEAR, Introduction to the Creeds, p. 248.

§ 2. The Church Doctrine.

Definition of Sin.

The Church doctrine defines sin, in accordance with 1 John 3:4, "as a deviation from the divine law" (Hollaz), a definition which is involved in the definition of others, that "sin is illegality", "contrary to law", "transgression of law", "contralegality or disconvenience with the law", or "discrepancy from the law".

Hollaz consequently defines sin thus: "Sin formally consists in the privation of conformity with the divine law, which law man is under obligation to obey". This includes the habitus, or tendency, as well as the act.

Further Explanations.

1) The cause of sin. "The cause of sin", says the Augsburg Confession, Art. XIX., "is the will of the wicked, that is, of the devil and ungodly men; which will, unaided of God, turns itself from God, as Christ says (John 8:44): "When he speaketh a lie, he speaketh of his own".

The true force of the words in this article is, not that God withholds his aid, and in consequence the wicked sin, but, that God gives no aid in the commission of sin. In a word, it means that sin originates in the self-determining power of the will, or, as we might say, in the self-averting power of the will.

2) God is not the author of sin. God is therefore in no sense the author of sin, not even *per accidens*. God tempteth no man, James 1:13. This is in no way contradictory to what Scripture says of God's hardening men. "God", says Hollaz, "does

not harden men causally or effectively, by sending hardness into their hearts, but judicially permissively, and desertively. For hardening is a judicial act, in which, on account of the preceding voluntary and avoidable evil, God justly permits a man, habitually bad, to rush into heavier crimes, and removes from him his grace, and finally delivers him to the power of Satan, by whom he is more and more impelled into greater sins, until he falls finally from all right to the heavenly inheritance".

3) The seat of sin. The primary seat of sin is in the soul, with its faculties acts, and habits. The secondary seat of sin is the body, because of the personal union of the body with the soul.

4) Sin is voluntary. If it be asked whether sin is in its essential nature voluntary, the reply is, that if the term voluntary be taken in its widest and its strictest sense, so as to cover the condition of the will as a faculty, as well as its acts all sin is voluntary, that is, inasmuch as it is connected either with a depraved act of the will, or with that depraved state of the will from which evil acts proceed. In this sense original sin, the sin of an infant, is voluntary. The will of an infant is depraved, and that condition of will pertains to original sin.

If however the word voluntary is limited so as to mean only that which is done with deliberate and conscious will, then it is not true that all sin is voluntary. It is evident, however, that this latter limitation is not a just one.

On this basis the Romish and Socinian or Unitarian view, which limits sin to the voluntary transgression of the law, does away with the reality of the sinfulness of original sin, and this fallacy is at the root of a great deal of New England Theology, which really simply repeats with some ingenuity and brilliancy the ideas of Plagiarism.

If a voluntary act of sin is sin, the condition of the will

which is antecedent to the act, and without which the act would not be, must also be sinful. The moral condition of the will precedes and determines its acts. While a will is holy in condition, it is impossible that it should be unholy in act. The act is what the condition is. Essential sin never comes to being in the thought or act, but is, and must be, in being before there can be a sinful thought or sinful act. The thought or act is not the root of sin, but sin is the root of the thought and act. The sin is really in the condition of the will. As Luther says: "Original sin, or sin of nature, sin of person, is the real cardinal sin. Did it not exist, no actual sin would exist. It is not a sin which is done, like all other sins, but it is, it lives, and does all sins, and is the essential sin".

5) The objective aim of sin. That which man reaches after in sin is always some thing conceived as good. Nothing can be desired by man simply considered as evil. It is always what in reality he thinks is a kind of good. The depraved desire of man is not born to evil as evil, but to some good, real or fancied, some advantage, some pleasure, some ease, which he supposes it will bring. Even when a man is said to do evil for the love of it, if we analyze the proposition it means he does evil because his depraved nature finds its comfort and satisfaction in the evil.

6) The consequence of sin. The consequence of sin is *reatus culpae*, liability of blame, and *reatus poenae*, liability to penalty.

The liability of blame is that obligation or binding condition, whereby man, on account of action, in conflict with the moral law or ont of conformity to it, is held, as it were, bound under sin and the impurity which clings to the sinner, so that because of that act he is regarded and styled a detestable sinner.

The *reatus poenae* or liability to penalty is that obligation or binding condition, whereby the sinner is held bound by God, the angered judge, to sustain the vengeance for unforgiven sin (Hollaz).

Recent Views of Sin.

1) Luthardt: Sin is a matter of the will, consequently of the personal nature of man, not as rationalism maintains, a matter simply of his sensuous nature, though this latter view has been held by many writers of higher order than mere rationalists, as by Rothe and Schleiermacher.

2) This rationalistic view is hut seemingly supported by the biblical doctrine of the flesh (*sarx*); for it is confuted by passages such as Gal. 5:20; 1 Cor. 1:26; 2 Cor. 1:12 ("fleshly wisdom"); Col. 2:18, 23 ("asceticism"); as well as by the demon-like essence of sin. This view would make God himself the author of sin.

3) Sin is not the result simply of the finite nature of man, the finiteness isolating itself from the whole, which is the pantheistic view.

4) It is not as the Hegelian School contends, the steps of the internal self-dualizing of the finite spirit, through whose division and conflict everyone must pass.

5) But it is, as Julius Mueller, Thomasius, Philippi, Kahnis and Luthardt maintain, the will of self-seeking, which regards the world not in its relation to God, but to the will itself.

6) The operation of sin is guilt, which implies accountability, obligation and objective relation of responsibility to the divine judgment. This reflects itself in the consciousness of guilt and is consummated in the penalty of death.

Historical Note on Recent Theories.

The work of Julius Mueller.

This is the greatest work as regards depth of thought and speculative power that has ever been written on the special subject of sin, and the first three books of the five under which the subject is discussed is a remarkable product of close reasoning and of biblical and philosophical scholarship. It is in the latter part of the fourth book, where he treats of hereditary sin and the origin of inborn sinfulness, that his speculations lead him astray, and he argues in favor of the theory of Pre-existence of the soul to explain the problem of hereditary guilt, thus condemning the favored theory of the Reformed theologians Creationism) and the theory of Traducianism, which most easily explains the problem of hereditary sin, and has been adopted by all the orthodox Lutheran divines.

Analysis of Book I. of Christian Doctrine of Sin.

THE REALITY OF SIN.
  Part I. The Nature of Sin.
  I. Sin as transgression of the Law.
    1) The fact of evil.
    2) Evil as opposition to Law.
    3) Is all evil a violation of the moral Law?
    4) Are there works of Supererogation, going beyond the demands of the Law?
    5) Is everything that falls short of the Law evil?
    6) Does the law precede or follow evil?

2. Sin as disobedience against God.
1) Kant's autonomy of the Will.
2) The elements of personality, self-consciousness and self-determination.
3) Proofs that the Law necessarily points to God.
4) Meaning of the word "sin", and Greek and Hebrew names.
3. Sin as Selfishness.
A. The Real Principle of the Moral Law.
1) Evil presupposes good.
2) Real principle of the Law identical with its motive, Love to God.
3) A system of Ethics based on the principle of Love.
B. The Real Principle of Sin.
1) Man's estrangement from God the primary sin and source of all other depravity. The innermost essence of sin is selfishness.
2) Distinction between self-love and selfishness.
3) Testimonies confirming the idea that selfishness is the root of sin.
(1) Scripture,
(2) The Fathers,
(3) The Reformers.
4) Derivation of the various forms of sin from selfishness.
5) Habitual and Actual Sin.

THE ESSENTIAL CHARACTER OF SIN,
Part II. The imputation of Sin.
1. Guilt and the Consciousness of Guilt.
1) Distinction between good and evil; guilt.
2) Degrees of guilt.
3) The consciousness of guilt.

2. Man's guilt and his dependence upon God.
1) The sense of sin and its guilt, and the problem suggests.
2) The providence of God.
3) The witness of Scripture concerning our guilt.
4) The doctrine of final judgment implies guilt.
5) Redemption implies human guilt.
6) Historical theories concerning guilt.
1) Early Fathers,
2) Scholastics,
3) The Reformers.

This valuable Discussion with his Introduction covers 267 pages of the first volume of his Christian Doctrine of Sin. We have here to do especially with the second of the five books embraced in his treatise, and presenting

An Examination of the Principal Theories in Explanation of Sin.

After a brief introduction, in which he calls our attention to the fact that this great problem has ever occupied the thoughts, not only of theologians and philosophers as their proper study, but also of all who have felt any desire to fathom the true significance of life, he discusses the subject under the following heads.

ANTHROPOLOGY

Derivation of Sin from the Metaphysical imperfection of Man.

1) Outline of this view as developed by Leibnitz in his *Theodicee*.

2) This view opposed to the phenomena of experience, to conscience and Scripture.

3) The doctrine of evil as privation is inadequate.

4) So the privative view of evil by the Early Fathers. Stress must also be laid on concupiscence as in our Confessions.

Derivation of sin from Man's sensuous nature.

1) Statement of the theory, which is only a form of the theory of privation, for it resolves itself into the weakness of the will as the seat of sin.

2) New development of this theory, making the spirit simply a development of nature, is in irreconcilable contradiction to experience.

3) If this theory is tested by the phenomena of sin, it is found that all sins springing from pride are ignored.

4) This theory has many points of coincidence with Pelagianism and strongly tends to Manichaeism.

5) Bearing of Scripture upon this theory.

(l) Christ's words are against it.

(2) Paul's general teaching opposed to this view.

(3) His doctrine of the Resurrection opposed.

(4) His doctrine concerning Christ opposed.

(5} The doctrine of the *sarx* opposed.

(6) Paul's conception of *sarx* goes far beyond man's sensuous nature.

6) Appendix. Kant's view of the origin of evil, compared with the theory of the derivation of sin from sense.

Schleiermacher's view of the essence and origin of sin.

1) Does Schleiermacher derive sin from man's sensuous nature?
(1) To say so is somewhat inexact, but there is foundation for this interpretation, since there is—
(2) Want of perspicuity in his statements.
(3) Indistinctness in his view of sin itself.
2) Schleiermacher resolves sin into the consciousness of sin.
(1) This theory is erroneous.
(2) He distinctly forbids any appeal to the freewill of the creature in deciding the question as to the ultimate ground of sin.
(3) With him, the feeling of freedom is nothing more than a determination of the sensuous self-consciousness.

His theory of the relation of sin to God.

(1) Sin is merely negative.
(2) This view leads to Pelagianism.
(3) He tries to avoid this issue.
(4) He virtually denies that sin is sin; for according to him, there must be sin, in order that the perfect development of the God-consciousness in us may be regarded as Redemption.
(5) Sin implies guilt only when subjectively viewed.
(6) His main error lies in his regarding the relation of created

personality to the uncreated as one of absolute dependence, and the relation of uncreated personality to the creature as one of absolute causality.

Derivation of evil from the contrasts of individual life.

1) Statement of this theory.
   (1) There are contrasts in nature;
   (2) In individual existence;
   (3) So between good and evil;
   (4) This simply evolves individuality;
   (5) Angels and the devil are mere personifications;
   (6) Good needs evil to give it reality and vigor;
   (7) Man must taste of evil in order to know and truly to choose the good;
   (8) This theory even holds that the nature of evil, the experience of individuals and of nations confirm it;
   (9) These contrasts and variations are indispensable;
   (10) This theory even tries to explain exceptions.

2) Historical account of this theory.
   (1) This theory held in ancient times.
   (2) This theory of evil is in its essence as much akin to Dualism as to Pantheism.
   (3) This theory has been carried to its extreme length in modern times.
   (4) Virtually adopted by many.

Two truths hostile to this theory.

(1) Our moral life is complete in itself according to God's original ordainment, 'Without requiring evil as its complement.

(2) Sin is not something isolated and merely out· ward, but an operative principle whose hindering and perverting influence pervades man's entire being, as seen in the awful ramifications of evil.

4) The strength of sin and its tyranny in the race.

5) Evil in its relation to the race as a whole.

We conclude this part of the discussion with the striking remark of Nitzsch: "The dogmatic assertion that good requires evil for its glorification is no less objectionable than the ethical maxim, 'let us do evil that good may come', Rom. 6:1".

The Hegelian theory of evil.

(1) Meaning of his definition, Evil is "the, first stepping forth of the spirit from its naturalness".

(2) With him evil ought not to be, but must exist in virtue of a higher speculative and logical necessity.

(3) Hegel does not hesitate to affirm that the variance of man with himself, in which evil consists, belongs to the true conception of man. "Man must eat of the tree of knowledge of good and evil, otherwise he would not be man, but an animal only".

(4) His view of the necessity of evil differs from Spinoza's view.

a) With Hegel, evil exists only because good requires it.

b) With Spinoza, what is called evil has its appropriate place by the same necessity as that which requires good.

(5) The metaphysical and the moral contradict each other; what the one demands, the other excludes.

(6) The moral necessity is destroyed by the metaphysical.

(7) Upon this principle of the necessity of evil the conception of guilt in its true import cannot be entertained.

(8) The maxim "evil a means of good" unsound.

(9) Upon Hegel's theory evil is necessary for the "process" of the Divine Life.

(10) A sinless Christ, as an historical individual, is impossible upon Hegel's theory.

(11) Evil is throughout regarded as wholly insignificant and weak.

(12) According to his theory the Christian doctrine of Redemption as a whole, if not altogether rejected must submit to a complete distortion.

Dualistic derivation of evil.

1) Dualistic theories alien to the spirit of our times.

(1) The Manicheans of ancient times attributed evil substance.

(2) Persian Dualism had its two opposite principles.

2) The notion of an original evil self-contradictory.

"From the time when the author sat as a scholar at the feet of the beloved Neander, the conclusion has been deeply rooted in his mind, that Christianity is a practical thing, that everything in it is connected more or less directly with the great facts of Sin and Redemption, and that the plan of Redemption which is the essence of Christianity, cannot be rightly understood until the doctrine of Sin be adequately recognized and established". (Julius Mueller.)

Divisions.

Indwelling sin reveals itself in particular internal or external acts of sin, which, according to the degree in which there is participation of the conscious will, involve divine grades of guilt and may rise to the height of unpardonable sin-the sin against the Holy Ghost.

The topic will be discussed under the two headings:
1. The General Definition of Sins of Act;
2. Divisions of Sins of Act.
§ 1. The General Definition of Sins of Act.

The Inner Principle Underlying Actual Sin.

In our former presentation we have seen that estrangement of man from God is the primary sin and the source of all other depravity. The Apostle Paul in Rom. 1:21-23 derives the awful degradation of the heathen, sunk in vices of all kinds, from their apostasy from the worship of the true God, and he describes as a righteous judgment of God the condition of those who will not hold fellowship with Him and can no longer maintain the supremacy of the spirit over nature, but sink into the most ignominious servitude to fleshly lusts. The immediate punishment of their apostasy consists in their becoming the prey of vile affections (Rom. 1:25, 26).

Sins of Act a Willful Turning Away From God.

Our conscience demands holiness and a loving submission to God, but this is put aside with aversion. Sin thus appears as it really is, a turning away from God. And while our guilt is enhanced, there ensues a benumbing of the heart resulting from the crushing of higher impulses. This constitutes the reprobate state of those who reject Christ and will not believe the Gospel. Upon the disappearance of the divine principle, there immediately ensues the entrance of a principle opposed to God, according to the saying of Christ, "he who is not with me is against me". Man cannot abandon his true relation to God, without setting up an idol in God's stead.

Selfishness is the Principle Underlying all Sins of Act.

We have already seen that selfishness is the inner, most essence of rain, the ruling and penetrating principle in all its forms. The idol which man in sin sets up in the place of God is none other than himself. In his inmost heart the sinner lives a life of selfish isolation, he stands alone in the world, shut up within himself, a chaos of selfish endeavors and preferences, without any true participation in the joys and sorrows of mankind, and in addition to all this, estranged from God.

Definition of Actual Sin.

Actual sin is to be distinguished from habitual or original sin in that it is the deflection of human acts from the rule of the divine law. Actual sins are so styled, because they are acts prohibited by the divine law, and are either of commission or omission. Actual sin is taken either in a looser and more general sense for all inordinate emotions or acts proceeding from original sin, or more strictly and specifically for single actions performed with a deliberate design of the mind and the definite malice of the will. In the second sense sins are not committed by the regenerate. A man must either be out of grace utterly or have fallen from it in order to commit this class of sins. This is the sense of 1 John 3:9. Neither can actual sin be committed by infants (Rom, 9:11).

How called in Scripture.

Actual sins are called works of the flesh, Gal. 5:9; unfruitful works of darkness, Eph. 5:11; deeds of the old man, Col. 3:9; dead works, Heb. 6:1; 9:14; lawless deeds, 2 Pet. 2:8. (Quenstedt.)

§ 2. Division of Sins of Act.

Actual sins are divided: With respect to cause, into voluntary and involuntary sins.

Voluntary sin is committed by a man knowingly and willingly and contrary to conscience. This can be done out of pure malice or wickedness, and with the will completely free, or it may be done under ensnaring cooperation from without. Voluntary sin falls even upon the renewed so far as, being overcome by depraved desire, they fall from a state of grace.

Involuntary sin is committed when there is not a certain knowledge nor a deliberate purpose of the will, and is either a sin of ignorance, or a sin of precipitancy, or a sin of infirmity.

Our Dogmaticians speak of a fourfold sin against conscience. (1) Against a correct conscience. A man sins thus when he despises the dictates of a conscience that agrees with the divine law, and sins against it either by acts of commission or omission. (2) Against an erroneous conscience. This occurs when by either action or omission, he turns away from a dictate of conscience imbued in error. (3) Against a probable conscience. One sins in this form when he goes contrary to the dictate of the intellect and conscience for probable reasons. (4) Against a doubtful conscience, in which case a man does or omits to do, that of which he is in doubt.

The Dogmaticians likewise have a two-fold division of voluntary sin in respect to the purpose of the will; the one kind of mere malice, and the second that which is committed under the power of a will influenced by force or fear, and by surrounding dangers, as in the case of Peter's denial (Matt. 26:70-74).

Of voluntary sins, we may say that, if consciousness of the act as a violation of God's law wanting in consequence of the darkness of the mind; which has not been yet entirely removed by the illumination of the Holy Spirit, it is a sin of ignorance. If the act of the will prompting to the sin be wanting, it is sin of precipitance, the excessive violence of the impulse, not suffering the will to discharge its office. The older dogmaticians call such sins as overtake the regenerate without any certain purpose of sinning, including sins of precipitance, sins of infirmity, defining them as "such sinful emotions of the mind which have suddenly arisen without the will, and whatever unlawful words or deeds which are the result of inadvertence or precipitancy, and are contrary to the purpose of the will".

They cite such cases, as the drunkenness of Noah, Gen. 9:21; the sin of Sarah in giving Hagar to Abraham as his wife, 16:1-5; Sarah's laughing at a promise of a child in her old age, 18:12; Moses' smiting the rock, Num. 20: 11, 12; the contention between Paul and Barnabas, Acts 15:39; when we do what we would not, Rom. 7:15; Peter's dissimulation at Antioch, Gal 2:11-14; being overtaken in a trespass, Gal. 6:1.

But Julius Mueller objects to the sins of precipitancy being included with sins of infirmity, for rightly they are a class of their own, or else we would have to regard a sin of infirmity as in kind a sin of premeditation, committed in opposition to a better prompting of the will, by reason of the weakness of this prompting and the strength of the temptation.

With respect to the person sinning, into mortal and venial sins, into sins of others and our own.

1) Hollaz's definition of mortal sin: Mortal sin, that in which they that have been renewed, being overcome by the flesh, contrary to the dictates of conscience, with deliberate purpose of evil, transgress the divine law, and in so doing show, that they have lost saving faith, throw aside the grace of the Holy Spirit, and plunge themselves into a state of wrath, death, and condemnation.

2) Hollaz's definition of venial sin: Venial sin is every involuntary sin in the renewed, which neither throws aside the

indwelling grace of the Holy Spirit nor extinguishes faith, but has conjoined with it, by an indissoluble connection, pardon in the very moment in which it is committed.

3) In and of themselves all sins are mortal, no sin is venial, and against this it is true that every sin is venial through Christ. The distinction of sin as mortal or venial arises

(1) From the different conditions of the person sinning, whether it be a renewed or an unregenerate;

(2) From the estimate which God has made in the Gospel, for God does not impute sins of infirmity, precipitance, and ignorance to the renewed for guilt and punishment;

(3) From the result in the different cases, for a mortal sin brings wrath, death, and condemnation, but a venial sin has pardon as an inseparable attendant, and man loses not the grace of God and saving faith.

4) As the causes of forgiveness of venial sins our dogmaticians name: the compassion of God, the satisfaction and intercession of Christ (1 John 2:1, 2; Rom. 8:1), the efficacious operation of the Holy Spirit, and the daily penitence of the renewed.

5) The right to make this distinction between particular sins is based upon 1 John 5:16.

6) In the Middle Ages they counted seven deadly sins, which Lombard regards as the seven fountains full of corruption and death to the soul. They were Pride, Covetousness, Luxury, Envy, Gluttony, Anger, and Sloth. . .

7) The Roman Church enumerates a series of sinful acts as deadly sins, in which a man does not indeed lose faith but loses the grace of justification.

8) The Protestant Church makes the distinction, not in the external act as such, but in the condition of mind and

in the person. It does not make a catalog and say, these are mortal , and another catalog and say, these are venial. On the contrary it acknowledges that all sin is in its own nature mortal. It acknowledges that the very same sin, as to its outward part, may be mortal to one person under a certain set of circumstances, and venial in another under a wholly different set of circumstances, e. g., open blasphemy of God on the part of one who had been an eminent saint, and blasphemy equally gross on the part of one who had never had opportunity to emerge from the crime in which he was reared from infancy. We all feel the difference, and would condemn with our bitterest reproaches in one, what we would look upon as a matter of sadness rather than of deep guilt in another.

9) The principle holds good in regard to sin, that the higher a man is in moral advantage the more grievous is the offence committed. Our Lord makes this distinction John 15:22. The regenerate man as such commits no mortal sin, only so far as he falls from grace. There are sins of infirmity in the regenerate, which are called venial sins and which do not remove the state of grace; on the other hand there are other sins which completely take it away.

10) The sin of another may be justly imputed to us when we concur by efficacious intention. Hollaz explains:—He concurs in the sin of another, who commands, consults, connives at, does not oppose, or gives information, and thus is the moral cause of the sin of another. He cites Eph. 5:7, 11; 1 Tim. 5:22; 2 John 11; and Rev. 18:4.

With respect to the sinning person into sins of the heart, lip and hand, or will, word and deed. The definition of Hollaz: "Sins of the heart are depraved thoughts and desires which are cherished within the human breast; sins of the lips are wicked words and gestures expressed by the lips; sins of deed are actions which are performed contrary to the divine law, by an external effort of the members. Matt. 5:21, 22.

With respect to the acts, into sins of commission and sins of omission.

1) Sins of commission are positive acts, by which the negative precepts of God are violated.

2) Sins of omission are the neglect of acts prescribed by the affirmative precepts of God; James 4:16, 17. (Hollaz.)

With respect to the object, into sins against God, sins against our neighbor and sins against ourselves. The chief passage, Tit. 2:12, in a general way may be regarded as placing Christian duties under three aspects, to ourselves, to others, and to God.

With reference to the effect into crying sins and sins that are not crying. Crying sins are those iniquities which call for and demand the vengeance of God; those that are not crying have not this flagrant character. According to Scripture the following are crying sins:

(1) The fratricide committed by Cain, Gen. 4:10;

(2) The sins of the Sodomites, Gen. 18:20;

(3) The oppression of the Israelites in Egypt, Ex. 3:9;

(4) The oppression of widows and orphans, Ex. 22:22;

(5) The denial of wages to the laborer, James 5:4.

The distinction has little dogmatic importance; it is rather rhetorical and popular than strictly scientific.

With respect to their adjuncts, into heavier and lighter sins, hidden and open, dead and hiding, abiding and forgiven, conjoined with hardness and free from hardness, pardonable and unpardonable. Sins are called heavier and lighter because of the weightier or lesser blame or violence attached to them.

Hollaz names five reasons why one sin is more grievous than another.

(1) In respect to the person sinning. A Christian sins more grievously than an unbeliever, though he commit the same crime.

(2) In respect to the impelling cause. He who commits adultery for the sake of gratifying his lust, sins more grievously than he who steals when impelled by hunger.

(3) In respect to the object. He is more guilty who slays his father than he who kills an enemy.

(4) In respect to the Law. He sins more grievously who violates his duties to God than he who violates the duties of the second table.

(5) In respect to the effect. That sin is regarded as the more grievous which is attended with the greater injury.

Hollaz: "A hidden or secret sin is that which is either unknown to the person himself who sins, or which is known only to him who sins, and a few others who wish it suppressed. An open sin is that which has become known to many, and, if it be connected with offence to others, is called a scandal. A scandal is an open sin which furnishes an occasion of sinning to those who know it".

Dead sins are those which indeed remain in us, but are not known as sins, or certainly not considered as great as they really are. Living sins are those which are known to be such, and rage even after the knowledge of the law, Rom. 7:8, 9.

An *abiding sin* is that which yet oppresses the sinner by its guilt and weight. A forgiven sin is that whose guilt has been removed from the sinner, by the grace of God, for the sake of the merit of Christ.

Hollaz: "Sin, connected with hardness of heart, is the most atrocious of all, by which the mind of man, having been polluted, remains averse to the Word of God and blind; the will, confirmed in wickedness, resists the Holy Spirit; the appetite indulges in beastly pleasures; and therefore the sinner, brings upon himself temporal and eternal punishment.

(1) The cause of this hardness is not God, but partly the devil, who multiplies evils, blinds the mind, and fills the heart with wickedness, 2 Cor. 4:4; Acts 5:3; Eph. 2:2; partly man, who rejects the ordinary means of salvation, and is continually selling himself to the desire and practice of sin, Matt. 13:15".

(2) With reference to Ex. 7:3, Hollaz remarks: "God does not harden men causally or effectually, by sending hardness into their hearts, but judicially, permissively, and by forsaking them.

Pardonable or remissible sins are those which, as they do not in their nature exclude repentance, can be and are wont to be forgiven or remitted. Irremissible or unpardonable sins are those which in their own nature are conjoined with permanent impenitence and on this account are never remitted or forgiven. Only sin which in its own nature precludes the possibility of repentance, and which necessitates a final impenitence, is unpardonable, and is to be distinguished from unforgiven sin, which includes every sin not actually forgiven.

The Sin Against the Holy Ghost.

The unpardonable sin is usually identified with the sin against the Holy Ghost. Sin against the Holy Ghost is defined as the malicious denial of the truth clearly known and veritably acknowledged and approved in the conscience, yet fought against and blasphemed, accompanied with an obstinate and final rejection of all the means of salvation. On this sin compare Matt. 12:31, 32; Mark 3:28, 29; Luke 12:10; Heb. 6:4-6; 10:26, 29; 1 John 5:16.

Quenstedt: The form of the sin against the Holy Ghost consists:

(1) In a denial, by a full, free, and unimpeded exercise of the will, of evangelical truth, after the latter has been evidently and sufficiently acknowledged and approved. Heb. 6:4; 10:26, 29.

(2) In a hostile attack upon the same. Matt. 12:31, 32.

(3) In voluntary and atrocious blasphemy. Heb. 10:26, 29.

(4) These three requisites of this sin must always be taken conjointly, and never separately, and then that must be called the sin against the Holy Ghost, concerning which all these can be conjointly verified.

As adjuncts of this sin Quenstedt names:

(1) Final impenitence, Heb. 6:4-6.

(2) Absolute irremissibility, Matt. 12:31; Mark 3:28, 29; Luke 12:10.

(3) Exclusion from the prayers of believers, 1 John 5:16.

Hollaz explains why the sin is not forgiven. "It is irremissible, not through any want of divine grace, or inadequacy of the atonement of Christ, or any want of the efficacious influence of the Holy Ghost, but on account of a wicked rejection of all means of grace, and by reason of final impenitence."

The presentation by Julius Mueller.

(1) The New Testament implies that this sin can only be committed as the extreme goal of a depraved development which has already passed through many stages of sin; of a degeneracy which has reached its acme. The sin implies a certain moral state in the person who commits it, the state of total obduracy.

(2) Christ does not represent it as a particular kind of unpardonable sin, but distinguishes it from all other sins as the only unpardonable sin.

(3) The sin against the Holy Ghost presupposes a very full and thorough development of the moral consciousness, and we may add the religious consciousness likewise. It presupposes this as something experienced at an earlier period in the person's life. Before man can possibly commit this sin, evil must thoroughly have taken possession of him by a penetrating and spiritualizing the process, making sins more heinous, wickedness more thorough, and accountability far greater that otherwise they could have been. Blasphemy against the Holy Ghost is not only the greatest, it is the most spiritual of sins. Unthinking recklessness, as such, is wholly secure from the sin against the Holy Ghost.

(4) We must not give up the main features of the theory of the older Dogmaticians concerning the sin against the Holy Ghost. Its essence is hatred of whatever is known to be divine and godlike. The blasphemy is the expression of this hatred, but in a much profounder sense than would at first sight appear. The inner motive of this hatred is unbending selfishness—a selfishness which hates God and His holy law. The decisiveness of the opposition consists in the fact that the man is fully

conscious of it and deliberately persists in it.

(5) This sin against the Holy Ghost is only another form of "the man of sin", the opposer of all law, the culminating point of man's depraved development as the deification of confirmed egoism and self-glorification. "The man of sin" must necessarily be the blasphemer of the Holy Ghost, and signalizes himself as "the son of perdition", one who has irrevocably abandoned himself to perdition (2 Thess. 2:3, 4).

(6) This culminating point of sin, blasphemy against the Holy Ghost, depends upon and is connected with the highest revelation of God; it has become possible only through Christ, and the mission of the Holy Ghost proceeding from Him.

(7) Some of our earlier Lutheran divines as Hutter, Quenstedt, Baumgarten, and others, insist upon a close connection between the sin against the Holy Ghost and God's revelation in Christ; for they hold that it presupposes regeneration. Most of them, however, do not venture to make this a necessary requisite, as Gerhard, Baier, Koenig, Buddeus, and others, but affirm only that the sin implies the knowledge of evangelical truth by the enlightenment of the Holy Ghost.

(8) But this enlightenment cannot be distinguished from regeneration, and the coincidence between the two classes of theologians in their quotations from Scripture illustrative of this sin, shows that they agree. They almost unanimously regard Heb. 6:3-6, in connection with Heb. 10:26-31, as one of the chief texts explaining the nature of the sin. The words of the writer of the epistle clearly show that he is referring to persons who by regeneration had become partakers of Christ's redemption.

(9) The idea that regeneration is necessarily implied in the sin against the Holy Ghost involves an important truth. The

highest religious consciousness alone is capable of committing the greatest sin, and only that man can possess this highest consciousness who has experienced true fellowship with God. He only can blaspheme the Holy Ghost who has in some degree partaken of his influences.

(10) We have already stated what is required objectively in order to commit this sin. Subjectively it implies a deep conviction, previously possessed, of the power of God's revelation in Christ, and of the efficacy of God's Spirit among men. This higher degree of consciousness once possessed as a secret force may impel the man who resists the Holy Spirit to persevering resistance and his sin may be intensified so as to become at last positive hatred of God and of His redemptive work.

(11) From the declaration of Christ (Matt. 12:24-37) and the context, we cannot positively decide whether He considered that the blaspheming Pharisees had already committed the sin, or whether He meant simply to warn them against it. They evidently were in imminent danger of committing the sin. The passage in Hebrews does indeed affirm that the regenerate may fall into this sin against the Holy Ghost, but it does not say that it can be committed by the regenerate alone.

(12) Obduracy, as we have seen, implies the objective presentation of the Revelation of God in history; and, on the other hand, blasphemy against the Holy Ghost, the highest and deepest development of sin, implies the suppression of a movement of the inner life following upon the working of the spirit of grace.

(13) Christ describes blasphemy against the Holy Ghost as the sin which shall never be forgiven. Our earlier theologians rightly discerned the true reason of this unpardonableness. It is not that divine grace is absolutely refused to anyone who

in true penitence asks forgiveness for this sin, but he who commits it never fulfills the subjective conditions upon which forgiveness is possible, because the aggravation of sin to this determination destroys in him all susceptibility of repentance.

THE WAY OF RETURN TO GOOD IS CLOSED AGAINST NO ONE WHO DOES NOT CLOSE IT AGAINST HIMSELF.

6

Moral Bondage, or the Doctrine of Free Will

Divisions.

The presence of evil in human life as the positive antithesis of good, is a fact which cannot be denied. This antithesis to good exists not only as a fact of consciousness but is manifest to the eye of God Himself; for He it is who condemns evil by the voice of conscience and the world's judgment, and who is destroying it by His redemptive work in the hearts of all who yield to His gracious rule. Yet this very fact, that God condemns evil and negatives its power, witnesses that the antithesis is not caused nor ordained by Him. Sin is to be found only in the creature, and can have its being only through the creature.

As in consequence of sin the tendency of man's mind has become alien from God, he is of himself incapable of what is truly good, and his will is inclined to all evil. If freedom is the highest assertion of self, and if sin is in its essence selfishness, what else must sin be but an abuse of freedom. Our inquiry accordingly must now be directed to the freedom of the human will, the true conception of it, its inner power, and its connection with evil.

The discussion naturally falls into two divisions:
1. The Scripture Doctrine;
2. The Church Doctrine.

§ 1. The Scripture Doctrine.

The Moral Bondage of Sinful Man.

In the Holy Scripture the moral bondage of sinful man is taught in what is said of the *sarx* or flesh. Because of this every imagination of the thoughts of man's heart is only evil continually from his youth, Gen. 6:5; 8:21. Consequently a renewal in the very center of nature is necessary, Ez. 11:19; 36:26, 27 "A new heart will I give you, and a new spirit will I put within you; and I will take away the stony heart", etc; Ps. 51:10, "Create in me a clean heart, O God; and renew a right spirit within me". The conflict between the natural thought and the divine thought of salvation is dwelt upon in 1 Cor. 1:17-2:16; the conflict of the natural will and ability is presented in John 15:5, "Apart from me ye can do nothing"; and in Rom. 7:7-11; man must be awakened from spiritual death to a new life, John 5:21; Eph. 2:5; Col. 2:12; he must be delivered from the slavery of sin, John 8:36; Rom. 6:20; and only regeneration by God can change the heart, John 3:3, 5.

A Relative Morality can be Attained.

On the other hand, with this low view of human ability is connected in the Scripture the possibility of a relative morality (Gen. 4:7, "If thou doest well, shalt thou not be accepted"? Rom. 2:14-16). All human creatures have the same moral nature, all have come short of the glory of God, but relatively to each other some have come much farther short of it than others. There is in man a natural consciousness of God (Acts 14:15-17; 17:22-28; Rom. 1:18, 19). And men have conscience (Rom. 2:14-16).

The Bible however does not teach that apart from the grace of God revealed in His word and ordinances there is any fellowship of man with God. See John 3:19-21, "But he that doeth the truth cometh to the light, that his works may be made manifest, that they have been wrought in God"; 6:44, "No man can come to me, except the Father which sent me draw him"; 7:17, "If any man willeth to do his will, he shall know of the teaching"; 18:37, "Every one that is of the truth heareth my voice"; 10:26, "Ye believe not, because ye are not of my sheep"; 11:52; Matt. 15:13. See also in regard to those "in every nation that fear God" in Peter's word to Cornelius, Acts 10:35; and the parable of the sower, Matt. 13:3. In this last parable is implied that there are relative degrees of fitness for the reception of the word, but not that these degrees are independent of the grace of God. In the ground of the human heart the character of these differences is determined by the freedom of the will. Whatever there is of evil of character is of the man himself, whatever there is of good is of God.

§ 2. The Church Doctrine.

The Teaching of the Greek Fathers.

The tendency of doctrine among the Greek Fathers is to an unconscious Semi-Pelagianism, that God has made man free and controller of himself.

According to Clemens Alexandrinus (d. 220) every man, in accordance with his own nature, ought to cultivate the talents which God has given him, and in every man there is power to good which the grace of God comes to aid. Man is accountable for that sin alone, which proceeds from free choice.

According to Origen of Alexandria (d. 254) it is a part of Christian preaching that every rational soul has free choice and will. There is no accountability without liberty. Nevertheless, this liberty is only relative; every moral action is a mixture of free choice and divine aid. "If men were corrupt by nature, and could not possibly do good, God would appear as the judge, not of actions, but of natural capacities".

Irenaeus (d. 202), although opposed to speculation, insists upon the self-determination in the use of the freedom of the will, and holds the freedom of man is not only seen in his works, but also in his faith.

Gregory of Nazianzum (d. 390) interprets Rom. 9:16 as meaning not alone of him that wills and not alone of him that runs, but also of God who showeth mercy.

Chrysostom of Antioch (d. 407) in Hom, XVI. on Hebrews says: "It is necessary for us first to choose the good, and when we shall be chosen, then also He will bring in the things that belong to Him".

The Doctrine of the Latin Fathers.

The older Latin Fathers give more prominence to grace, and yet in such a way as to make the beginning of faith precede grace.

Even the austere Tertullian of Carthage (d. 220) defended the idea of liberty, especially in opposition to Marcion: "How could man, who was destined to rule over the whole creation, be a slave in respect to himself, and not have the faculty of reigning over himself".

Cyprian of Carthage (d. 258) says on the one side, everything that we can do is of God; that we should glory in nothing since nothing is our own. On the other side he says: "Just so much of capacious faith as we bring so much do we drink in of overflowing grace".

Ambrose of Milan (d. 397) also did not exclude the liberty of man from the work of moral reformation, but on the other hand he says, "the will is made ready", and the other Fathers also recognized the notion, wanting on the part of the Greek writers, of a prevenient, internal grace.

The ultimate consequence of the false views of freedom which were so prevalent, was reached by Pelagius and afterwards by Coelestius and bishop Julian of Eclanum, while Augustine came forth as the mighty defender of the doctrine of grace.

The Teaching of Pelagius.

Pelagius was a man whose development of life had been quiet. He was pure in morals, but destitute of all depth of experience, all profoundness of thinking, all deep consciousness of sin. He represents in his doctrine the superficial nature of the views of man when he rests in his own moral power. From the notion of formal freedom he deduces in the case of every man the possibility of deciding for good as well as for evil. He denies original sin and inherited guilt, and maintains that death would have necessarily been even without Adam's sin and that Adam himself, whether he bad sinned or not sinned, would have died. The universality of sin is the result of bad example and the preponderance of the sensual. Grace is in part, the adaptation to good itself, in part, the law, doctrine and example of Christ; it is an illumination of the understanding, not the principle of the will making a new creature.

He says:"There is in the first place possibility, in the second, volition, and in the third, actuality. We locate possibility in nature, volition in will, actuality in the effect. The first of these belongs to God, the two others are to be referred to man.—Free will always gives us the power of choosing one of two things since we always are able to choose either.—I affirm a man can be without sin and can keep the commands of God.—Every good or bad tiring whereby we become worthy either of praise or censure does not take its origin with us but is done by us. We have capacity for either; we are not born with powers, and as we are propagated without virtue so also " without vice, and before the action of our own wills, that alone is in man which God has formed". Pelagius taught that Christians had the aid of the grace of God, which however consisted in the teaching and example of Christ so that what men are commanded to do of their own free will, they can more easily fulfil by grace. God assists us by His teaching and by His revelation.

The Teaching of Augustine.

Over against these views of Pelagius, Augustine with great power, yet not without some of those extravagances into which ardent minds are apt to fall in heated controversies, maintained that humanity is a mass of perdition" with "a miserable necessity of sinning". "Adam was, and in him we all were, Adam perished, and in him all perished". He maintained that free will "is free to sin because it is the slave of sin". Apart from grace there is nothing but splendid vices, no genuine good work, for where love is not there is no good work"—"Grace precedes our willing and makes willingness out of unwillingness. It precedes the unwilling so that he does will. It follows the willing so that he does not will in vain". He speaks of the inspiration or inbreathing "of good will and working or of the inspiration of love". "God sues, but so that he may persuade. God works in man the very willingness to believe.

The calling is that which effects the good will". "No man resists God's will to save him". Augustine consequently teaches an irresistible and particular grace. No creaturely will can resist the almighty will of God. To the elect who are called in accordance with their election, God gives the gift of perseverance, not only because without that gift they could not but persevere.

Semi-Pelagianism.

Between these two tendencies stood the Semi-Pelagians. If they attempted to relieve the two extremes of Augustinianism and Pelagianism. They were also called Massilians, and among them were John Cassian and Faustus of Rhegium. The doctrine of the latter was assailed by Hilary and Prosper, who characterize it as a shapeless third, something which it was difficult to recognize. This tertium or shapeless third consisted in the following particulars:

1) The natural man is neither morally healthy, as Pelagius thought, nor morally dead (Augustine), but diseased and morally weakened;

2) Freedom and grace concur, sometimes the one leading, and again the other; the initiation is usually in the will;

3) The rejection of the doctrine of predestination, in the sense of Augustine.

The Work De Vocatione Gentium (On the Call of the Gentiles).

The writing *On the Calling of the Gentiles* (attributed by some to Leo),[35] a work of the middle of the fifth century, sought the middle way between Semi-Pelagianism and Augustinianism, by the supposition of a general grace, preparatory, in addition to the proper grace of salvation. "We believe that the aid of grace is not taken entirely from any man for grace is

---

[35] Editor's note: Scholars are now agreed that St. Prosper of Aquitaine authored this work while employed as Pope Leo's secretary.

multiform".

Condemnation of These Heresies.

The African Synod of Carthage (418) and of Milevis (416) rejected Pelagianism and Zosimus of Rome confirmed their decision 418 A. D. The Council of Ephesus (431) united in the condemnation without entering more deeply into the question. Semi-Pelagianism was rejected by the second Council of Orange (529) but that council also rejected the idea of predestination to evil and did not, at least expressly, teach the doctrine of irresistible and particular grace.

Roman Catholicism.

The theology of the Middle Ages tends more and more to Semi-Pelagianism and in part to Pelagianism, in order to make place for the doctrine of merit. By original sin "man is indeed wounded as regards natural good, but totally despoiled of those gratuitous gifts which through grace were added to the natural gifts" (Peter Lombard). Consequently, he needs healing grace. On this point Thomas Aquinas teaches more after the spirit of Augustine, though he also supposes the *meritum de congruo*, the merit which arises from a congruity · or adaptation to grace, of which man is the author.

Thomas Aquinas says: "It is the work of man to prepare his mind, because he does this by free will, yet this be does not without the aid of God, who draws him to himself, for God is, in general, the *primum movens*, is everything".

MORAL BONDAGE, OR THE DOCTRINE OF FREE WILL

Hereby man disposes himself (and in this consists the *meritum de congruo*) for the reception of habitual grace. In virtue of this, then, he is prepared to do good and to enjoy God (and herein consists the *meritum de condigno*, the merit of worthiness).

This implies that we obtain grace by the first merit and obtain the second merit by grace.

Duns Scotus starts with free will. Out of the power of free will grows the habitude of love, the condition of the mind antecedent to love and making it possible. This condition of the mind God regards as meritorious.

Grace then takes the attitude only of an assistant to this. "Man is adapted by his natural powers to believe and love, nevertheless he cannot without grace believe and understand love". "We so confess free will as to say that we always need the aid of God". "Although free will has great virtue in merit, yet without grace it is not sufficient for the salvation of man".

Gabriel Biel, following still further this line of thought, taught that man, if he follow the dictate of reason can of himself perform moral good can in fact love God supremely by his own powers. The moral good, however, becomes a meritorious good according to God's order, only through grace which renders man an object of favor. This was lost by man in original sin, for this it is which is the super-added gift of grace which man now by nature lacks.

Against this view Luther directed his polemic, fighting that Pelagianism which bad become almost universally triumphant in the Church of Rome, and there is no question that the polemic of the Reformers led to a moderation of this tendency in that church, but by no means to its complete extinction.

The Church of Rome still praises Augustine and follows

Pelagius. The Council of Trent VI. Chap. 1 says: "Free will is by no means extinct, though weakened in its powers". Canon 4: "If any one shall say that the free will of man, moved and excited by God, does not cooperate by assenting to God, who excites and calls, whereby he disposes and prepares himself to obtain the grace of justification, and that he holds himself merely passively,—let him be anathema". Canon 7: "If any one saith, that all works done before justification, in whatsoever way they be done, are truly sins, or merit the hatred of God: let him be anathema". Chapters 5 and 6 of the Decree on Justification describe at length how grace makes the beginning with the call, and how man yet must free concur and co-work. "They who by their sins were turned from God, may by His exciting and assisting grace be disposed, by freely assenting to that grace and cooperating with it, to turn themselves in order to their own justification; nevertheless without the grace of God, man cannot of his own free will move himself to righteousness before God".

Luthardt's judgment in regard to this, is: The freedom is Pelagian, and the grace is magical.

Protestantism.

The original Protestantism of the Reformation, in its consciousness of the deep corruption of our sinful nature, denies that there is a real moral freedom in divine things.

Luther acknowledges, indeed, that man of himself can render an obedience to the externals of the law. He says: "Are we then to condemn everything that we see in honorable moral people, who live chastely, correctly, obediently, and who do many good works after the law? Are not all these excellent gifts of God and commendable virtues? Answer, yes, this we also say and we would add that God has commanded this and will have man thus to live and be pious. But here the question is in regard to the heart which is the source and spring of the chief sins, as of false service of God, of contempt of God, of unbelief, disobedience, of evil desires, and striving against God's command, and, in brief, what Paul calls (Rom. 8) fleshly mindedness and which he characterizes as enmity against God, which is not subject to the law of God, neither indeed can be. Wherefore all that external piety and morality is of no value as regards the acceptance of man as God's child, because it does not proceed from a free, joyous heart and lacks love to God and to His law. It is the toil of the slave, not the work of the child".

With this Luther connected, especially in his earlier period, the doctrine that God is ultimately the only worker; that we are passive to God's workings and are only as an instrument in the hands of God. This he taught, in the disputation with Carlstadt, at Leipzig, 1519, and in his book, *De Servo Arbitrio*, 1525, On the Bondage of the Will. But as his theological views ripened under the influence of the Holy Scriptures, he more and more withdrew from the deterministic speculations in regard to the relation of the will of the creature to the Divine omnipotence, and confined himself to the purely ethical question in regard to the relations of the sinful will to divine grace. His doctrine is summed up very briefly in the words of the Small Catechism on Art. 3 of the Apostles' Creed: "I believe that I cannot by my own reason or strength believe in Jesus Christ my Lord, or come to him; but the Holy Ghost has called me through the Gospel, enlightened me by his gifts, and sanctified and preserved me in the true faith".

Melanchthon's view in his purest period is the same. According to him, original sin is "a living energy", in consequence of which there is "darkness in the mind, aversion from God in the will, inordinate and manifold self-love, and in the heart there is a depraved inclination, and a contumacy against sound judgment".—"Wherefore there is nothing in us but death and sin, therefore nature can do nothing but sin".

In regard to this moral want of freedom, Melanchthon also at the beginning had taught the deterministic theory, but as early as 1527 in his expositions of Epistle to the Colossians, he had set determinism aside.

The Augsburg Confession. In accordance with the ripest and fuller scriptural views of our Reformers, the Augsburg Confession thus expresses itself in Art 18. *On Free Will*:

I. Thetical statement:

1) They teach, that man's will has some liberty the attainment of civil righteousness, and for the choice of things subject to reason;

2) Nevertheless, it has no power, without the Holy Ghost, to work the righteousness of God, that is, spiritual righteousness;

3) Since the natural man receiveth not the things of the spirit of God 1 Cor. 2:14;

4) But this righteousness is wrought in the heart when the Holy Ghost is received through the Word;

5) So in substance the testimony of Augustine.

II. Antithesis:

1) They condemn the Pelagians and others who teach that, without the Holy Ghost, by the power of nature alone, we are able to love God above all things;

2) For, although nature is able in some sort to do the outward

work (for it is able to keep hands from theft and murder), yet it cannot work the inward motives, such as the fear of God, trust in God, chastity, patience, etc.

4) The Apology. Similar language is used in the Apology, Art. 18.

1) The human will has liberty in the choice of works and things which reason comprehends by itself.

2) Since there is left in human nature reason and judgment concerning objects subjected to the senses, choice between these things, and the liberty and power to render civil righteousness, are also left.

3) Although the power of concupiscence is such that men more frequently obey evil dispositions than sound judgment. And the devil, who is efficacious in the godless (Eph. 2:2), does not cease to incite this feeble nature to various offences.

4) These are the reasons why even civil righteousness is rare among men.

5) It is false that the man does not sin, who performs the work of the commandments without grace.

6) For human hearts without the Holy Ghost are without the fear of God, without trust toward God, do not believe that they are hearkened to, forgiven, benefited, and preserved by God, and are therefore godless (Matt. 7:18; Heb. 11:6).

7) Therefore, although we concede to free will the liberty and power to perform the outward works of the Law, yet to the free will we do not ascribe these spiritual matters,—truly to fear God, truly to believe God, truly to be confident and hold that God forgives us, etc. (1 Cor. 2:14).

8) Even for saints to retain this faith is difficult, so far is it from existing in the godless.

9) Thus a distinction is shown between human and spiritual

righteousness, between philosophical doctrine and the doctrine of the Holy Ghost, and it can be understood for what there is need of the Holy Ghost, for men cannot obey God's law without the Holy Ghost.

The Synergism of Melanchthon.

In 1535 Melanchthon began to teach that three causes of conversion should be combined, "the Word, the Holy Spirit and the Will, not entirely passive, but resisting its infirmity. These causes the ecclesiastical writers are accustomed to conjoin. Basil says, 'only will and God go beforehand'. God anticipates us, calls us, moves us, aids us, but let us see to it that we do not resist, Chrysostom says, 'He who is drawing, draws the willing'.—For we ought not to indulge natural diffidence or slothfulness.—I do not approve the frenzies of the Manichaeans, who attribute no action whatever to the will, not even when the Holy Spirit aids, as if there were no difference between a statue and the will".

In 1548 Melanchthon uses the Erasmian definition: "Free will is the faculty of applying oneself to grace". In the *Examen oridandorum* he says, "These causes concur in conversion, the Word of God, the Holy Spirit, and our will assenting to and not resisting the Word of God". These expressions of Melanchthon fail to answer the vital question, which is, whence has the will this assenting power, this applying itself to the grace of God?

Later Synergism.

Out of this later tendency of Melanchthon arose the doctrine of Synergism, the doctrine of the human will working conjointly with God as a cause of conversion, Its earliest distinct representative is Pfeffinger, 1555. He maintains that the will is "a concurrent cause", for we are fellow-workers with God. Strigel is more generally known as a synergist. In the Weimar Disputation, 1560, he maintains that man is a free agent analogous to God, the most free agent, and that consequently man must retain even in conversion a mode of acting correspondent to his free agency, a mode wherein he distinguishes himself from all the objects of nature. Hence follows the activity of the will in conversion. "The will acts in its own mode in conversion. In it it is neither a statue nor a stock. In its trembling it assents, at the same time seeking aid". At a later period Strigel taught more correctly that "free will is capacious of salvation, that the Holy Spirit through the Word restores to the will the power or efficacy or faculty of believing, which was lost in the fall".

Opposed by Flacius Illyricus.

Flacius resisted this synergistic tendency, giving prominence to the passiveness of man in conversion, the resistance of the natural will, and the sole activity of the Holy Spirit. He maintained that man, so far as the concurrence of his own will as the cause of conversion is concerned, "is thoroughly like a stock or statue, destitute of all understanding or power". In place of the image of God man now has the image of Satan.

Man is converted "not only without his natural free will co-operating of itself, hut on the contrary, with that will raging and striving against conversion". "To understand and will what is good" comes alone from conversion through the Holy Spirit Himself, and not until then does co-operation take place. Running out this tendency still further a few of our Dogmaticians went to extremes in the doctrine of particular grace. The decision of the points of controversy which had arisen among our own divines is found in Chapter II. of the Formula of Concord.

Teaching of Formula of Concord.

1. The question at issue.

1) This is not concerning the condition of free will of man before the fall;

2) Nor his ability since the fall, and before his conversion, in external things;

3) Nor his ability in spiritual things after he has been regenerated and is controlled by God's Spirit;

4) Nor the sort of a free will that man has after the resurrection of the body;

5) But what powers, in spiritual things, man has, from himself, since the fall, and before regeneration and whether, from his own powers, before he has been born again by God's spirit, he be able to dispose and prepare himself for God's grace, and to accept and apprehend or not, the grace offered through the Holy Ghost in the Word and holy Sacraments.

2. In reference to the knowledge of divine things it says: "Man has still indeed a dim spark of knowledge that there is a

God, as also al the doctrine of the law, Rom. 1:19, 20 (p. 553, 9); but in spiritual things, the understanding and reason of man are entirely blind, and, by their own powers, can understand nothing, 1 Cor. 2:14 (p. 497, 2)".

3. In reference to the will it says: "The will of unregenerate man is not only turned away from God, but also has become an enemy of God , so that it has inclination and desire for that which is evil and contrary to God, Gen. 8:21; Rom. 8:7; Eph. 2:5; 2 Cor. 3:5 (p. 497, 3); so that in spiritual and divine things the intellect, heart and will of the unregenerate man cannot, in any way, by their own natural powers, . . . will, begin, effect, do, work or concur in working anything, but they are entirely dead to good, and corrupt (John 8:34; Eph. 2:2; 2 Tim.. 2:26); . . . hence the natural free will, according to its perverted disposition and nature, is strong and active only with respect to what is displeasing and contrary to God (p. 552, 7)".

4. With respect to his conversion man is purely passive. "When Luther says that with respect to his conversion man is purely passive, that is, does nothing whatever thereto, but only suffers what God works in him, his meaning is not that conversion occurs without the preaching and hearing of God's Word, but he means that man of himself, or from his natural powers, cannot contribute anything or help to his conversion, and that conversion is not only in part, but altogether an operation, gift and present and work of the Holy Ghost alone, who accomplishes and effects it, by his virtue and power, through the Word, in the understanding, will and heart of man (p. 569, 89)".

5. The Holy Spirit effects conversion. "The Holy Ghost effects conversion, yet not without means, but uses for this purpose the preaching and hearing of God's Word, Rom. 1:16;

10:17 (p. 497, 4)".

6. Only two efficient causes in conversion. "Before the conversion of man, there are only two efficient causes, namely, the Holy Ghost and the Word of God, as the instrument of the Holy Ghost, whereby He works conversion (p. 500, 19); for the conversion of our corrupt will, which is nothing else than a resuscitation of it from spiritual death, is only and alone a work of God, just as also the resuscitation in the resurrection of the body should be ascribed to God alone (p. 569, 87)".

7. The natural man is spiritually dead. "The Scriptures teach that man in sins is not only weak and sick, but also entirely dead, Eph. 2:1, 5; Col. 2:13. As a man who is physically dead, cannot of his own powers, prepare himself to obtain again temporal life, so the man who is spiritually dead in sins, cannot of his own strength, prepare himself to the acquisition of spiritual righteousness and life (p. 553, 11)".

8. The natural man is worse than a stone or rough block, which resists only passively, not actively. "The free will, from its own natural powers, not only cannot work or co-work as to anything for its own conversion or believe or assent to the Holy Ghost, who through the Gospel offers him grace and salvation, but rather from its innate, wicked, perverse nature it hostilely resists God and His will, unless it be enlightened and controlled by God's Spirit. On this account the Holy Scriptures compare the heart of the unregenerate man to a hard stone, which does not yield to the one who touches it, but resists, and to a rough block, and to a wild unmanageable beast; not that man, since the fall, is no longer a natural creature, or is converted to God without hearing and meditating upon God's Word (p. 555, 18, 19); but when man despises the instrument of the Holy Ghost (the Word), and will not hear, no injustice

befalls him if the Holy Ghost do not enlighten him, but .he be allowed to remain in the; darkness of his unbelief, and to perish; . . . and in this respect it might well be said that man is not a stone or: block. For a stone or block does not resist that which moves it, and does not understand and is not sensible of what is being done with it, as a man, as long as he is not converted, with his will resists God the Lord. . . He can do nothing whatever for his conversion, and is in this respect much worse than a stone and block; for he resists the word and will of God, until God awakens him from the death of sin, enlightens and renews him (p. 563, 58, 59)".

Teaching of Lutheran Dogmaticians.

General presentation.

Our old divines teach, in strict accordance with the Symbolical Books, the doctrine of free will. They admit that in the natural man there may be in part a carnal *conatus* (effort) in reference to God's Word (Selnecker) or a general desire of salvation (Aeg. Hunnius) or a general knowledge of salvation, a confused cognition and a general pleasure or assent and simple complacency in the plan of salvation (Musaeus), all of which are consistent with a deep seated hatred to God in the inmost heart of man. There is no real desire, no true cognition, no genuine conformity of will. It is not that the nature of man lifts itself to the supernatural, but that it drags down the supernatural to the level of nature. But as regards the work of salvation, the power of man is limited to the faculty of hearing the Word with the outward ear (Hutter). The hearing of the Word and the like, was regarded in common with civil righteousness as belonging to the lower hemisphere in reference to which the natural man has free will. On the other hand it was held, that it belonged to the superior hemisphere "to go into the temple for the sake of receiving information from the preached word, to read and hear the Word of God with a desire of being profited, to be held by the wish of being informed from God's Word. All which things are the works of prevenient or incipient grace" (Koenig, Quenstedt).

Scientific presentation.

The question clearly stated.

(1) Chemnitz: This topic would have been more clearly stated concerning man's powers than concerning the freedom of the will.

(2) Gerhard: Two faculties belong to the rational soul, mind and will. The mind performs its office 1) by knowing, 2) by discriminating, 3) by reflecting, 4) by judging; the will 1) by choosing and 2) by rejecting. In free determination, which is a faculty of the mind and will, determination belongs to the mind, and free belongs to the will.

(3) Gerhard: The question is not whether man since the Fall has lost his will, for we maintain that man has not lost his will, but the soundness of it.

The natural will is free and voluntary after the Fall.

(1) Gerhard: It is not forced or violently hurried along to do anything contrary to its inclination—there is, therefore, freedom from compulsion;

(2) It does not act alone by natural instinct, so that the will has also freedom from inward necessity;

(3) It has interior liberty, and is moved voluntarily, and has within itself the principle of its own motion:

(4) There is liberty in the subject, for neither the will, nor the essential liberty of the will, has been lost by the Fall.

A true definition of liberum arbitrium, or free will.

(1) If with Hutter we define free will "to signify the capacity of determining freely to choose that which is good and freely to avoid that which is evil", we would deny that free will has remained in man since the Fall.

(2) For the natural man can no longer freely choose between good and evil, but on account of sin, both original and of act, has lost the power to will and to do that which is good.

(3) If, therefore, we understand free will or liberty as describing the free power and faculty of choosing the good and rejecting the evil, which was possessed by Adam before the Fall, we maintain that Luther was perfectly correct in saying, "Free will is a title without the thing itself , or a thing with nothing but a title" (Gerhard).

The natural man is completely destitute of free will in spiritual things.

(1) Chemnitz: The human will cannot, by its own powers, without the Holy Spirit, either begin interior and spiritual movements, or produce interior obedience of the heart.

(2) For such movements cannot be performed except by the agency of the Holy Spirit; and unrenewed nature cannot perform such actions, and even hinders the Holy Spirit in performing them.

(3) That such power is lacking Quenstedt proves as follows:
a) As to the intellect, Eph. 5:8; 1 Cor. 2:14;
b) As to the will, Rom. 8:7; 6:17, 20; Eph. 2:1, 2; Matt. 7:18.

There is, however, liberty of choice in regard to what is evil.

(1) Quenstedt: The natural man has liberty, not, indeed, that which is employed between spiritual good and evil, for this was lost by the Fall, but that which is employed between this and that spiritual evil in particular;

(2) Gerhard: This liberty is one of contradiction, when it is employed about one and the same object, and one sins freely and delights to sin, and chooses freely;

(3) This liberty is one of contrariety, when it is employed about diverse objects or about diverse acts of the same object, for in the very choice of evils, the natural man exercises a certain liberty.

There is also in the natural man a liberty of choice in external things.

(1) Chemnitz: From Rom. 1:20, it is very evident that the mind was not despoiled of all intellect by the Fall, but that there is remaining even in unregenerate men, some power of mind in perceiving and judging those things which have been subjected to reason and the senses, as in inventing and learning the various arts, in domestic life, politics, ethics, in counsel, prudence, etc.

(2) For proof Chemnitz gives two reasons: a) Paul affirms that there is a carnal righteousness, Rom. 2:14; 10:3; Phil. 3:6; b) Paul says that the Law is the object of free will, even among the unjust, 1 Tim. 1:9, that is, the Law was given to the unregenerate to restrain the will, the affections of the heart and locomotion in externals.

(3) Our later divines speak of two hemispheres, about which the will of man in the state of corruption is occupied, the lower and the higher. To the higher belong the things purely spiritual, in which the man in the state of corruption has no free-will, and cannot of his own ac cord even cherish a desire for salvation and a change of his present depraved condition.

To the lower hemisphere Hollaz refers "all things and actions 1 physical, ethical, political, domestic, artificial, pedagogic, and divine, as far as they can be known by the light of reason, and can be produced by the powers of nature aided by the general concurrence of God, . . . although that power is languid and infirm".

Period of Transition.

In the period of transition, especially subsequent to Buddeus (d. 1729), stress was laid upon the assertion that there are pedagogic acts and a certain prevenient grace, a general grace, forerunning grace, even outside of this sphere of the operations of, salvation, and thus a connection is furnished between the condition of the natural man and that of regeneration.

Rationalism, however, went beyond this into Pelagianism. As early as 1821 Sartorius renewed the Church doctrine of "the inability of the free will for a higher morality".

In his *Doctrine of Divine Love* he says (1842) "Human nature affected with sin, and thereby in bonds, cannot release itself, because only the free can liberate the enslaved; but it can be made free by redemption. The will cannot effect this redemption, for it needs itself to be redeemed from the service of selfishness, . . . for the habitual disposition and sinfulness of the natural man is selfishness".

According to Hase, Pelagius emphasized the moral interest, Augustine the religious, while the truth lies in the full unity of both. "So everything in the religious life is grace and everything is freedom, that is, freedom itself is the great gift of grace". In virtue of this, man can and should strive alter God.

According to Schleiermacher, the inworking of the religious life of the communion which goes forth from Jesus Christ,—this consciousness of God is exalted to the power in us which is decisive in its character, while previous to this inworking man can act only in detached impulses, and so is in no condition to break the communion of the flesh in himself, and has only the capacity of receiving for himself the grace which is offered.

This style of thinking became very prominent and may be called the modern form of synergism. It is represented in Nitzsch and Julius Mueller, who, on the basis of the power which remains to the natural man to follow the higher drawing in our nature, ascribes to him "the possibility of an independent and self-active relation to the operations of grace".

Martensen[36] speaks of an innate or a concrete grace, which is identical with essential freedom and which comes with a surrender of itself to grace, by a breaking through within the natural will. "It is immanent grace, in the yielding heart of man, which constrains free will to surrender itself to the grace which seeks an entrance, which enables it to open to its influence, like the flower which opens to the sunbeam".

Teaching of More Conservative Lutheran Theologians.

The most decided Church theologians of our day, as Thomasius, Kahnis, Frank, Luthardt, and others, reject this Synergism. They, however, not only demand that emphasis be given to the grace in conversion, on the ground of the internal,working of saving grace, but also recognize the possibility of a condition for preparation for the grace of salvation, on the ground of the universal working of God through the conscience and in other similar ways.

---

[36] Christian Dogmatics, 204.

Presentation by Harless, and the True Solution.

The most conservative and entirely scriptural presentation of this difficult problem is given by Harless, one of the greatest of modern dogmaticians and ethical writers in the Lutheran Church and of all times, an outline and summary of whose discussion we attempt here to present.

I. The Working of the Spirit of Regeneration on the Spirit of Man and on his Personal Consciousness.

1. When the Holy Spirit begins to operate through the Word in our spirit, in contrast with our natural condition, there begins in us a new relation and procedure of God towards us, which manifests itself in vital energy, in consequence of which a new course of conduct toward God on our part is rendered possible. As through the Holy Spirit and God's Word ("his precious and exceeding great promises") "we become partakers of the divine nature, having escaped from the corruption that is in the world" (2 Pet. 1:4), there thus begins to dwell within ourselves a divine ground for the determination of our conscious personal conduct.

1) In 2 Pet. 1:4, Peter mentions participation in the divine nature as the aim of the promises given to us. And this takes place only when that which God Himself is, has become the normal ground of our own nature. This is the communion of God Himself with us. It is the Father and the Son, who, in the communion of the Holy Ghost, take up their abode with us (John 14:23).

2) If, however, that which may be truly called the regenerating communion of God with us, can take place in us, then must it enter into the spiritual basis of our life and being, no matter whether I regard the hearing of the word, or the sacrament of

baptism (the sacrament of the new birth), as the means.

3) No matter in which way the new life has been implanted within man, that inward source of regenerating communion with God must become in the unconscious depths of our spirit a creative and impelling power, an evermore working power which rules us in the inmost depth of our existence. It makes itself felt as a power which comes upon me, and seizes my spirit,—not as a power which I consciously, and in the way of self-determination, impart to myself. My own action in this domain is only that of non-resistance and of receiving into the form of what is self-perceived, a power wrought even by the Holy Spirit, and not an action self-derived and self-determining.

4) The word heard is a faith-producing power, and faith is not a condition of the power of the word, but only the condition of the continuance of the blessed and saving operation of this power. There remains, under all circumstances, an act of God which lays hold of and quickens our spirit, and thus God regenerates me through His word, and not I myself through my faith. For true faith is never and in no case obtained, except in consequence of a spiritual quickening, which quickening does not spring from myself, but from God. It stands opposed to my natural knowledge and will and presents itself to my consciousness as an overpowering force. And this fact remains the same whether I regard this operation of God as effected either through the Word heard or through the sacrament of baptism received.

5) We are never to expect that the efficacy of the Holy Spirit, when He begins his work, is at once present in all His fullness. Christ, indeed, in all His fullness, stands over against us in His life-giving word, yet the full measure of His presence and

efficacy is given only in proportion to the faith in which I appropriate the Word to myself. The conscious will of the natural man is of such a nature that it closes as with bolts the approach to the inner man against that working of the Holy Spirit which comes upon him from without through the Word; so that only in proportion as these bolts one after another give way, does the efficacy of God the Spirit penetrate deeper and deeper into our inner man.

6) It is otherwise with the sacrament of baptism, the sacrament of the new birth or regeneration. There the fullness of God's fellowship with us, as it is appointed for us in this life, is bestowed as a free gift. The fountain of life sinks into our inmost man; and this full entrance of the fellowship of God with us is conditioned, not by the measure of our faith, but purely by the will of God touching His sacrament. By God's will this fellowship has fully taken place. Only the degree of its blessing depends on that of my faith, and my faith can only guard against the conversion of that blessing into a curse.

The connecting point for this working of God in and upon our human spirit, through the agency of the Holy Spirit, lies in our conscience. By virtue of this bond of communion we are joined to God in Christ, and are no longer under wrath, but under grace, and the Holy Spirit which giveth life is present to our spirit. And this is accomplished in us, without any cooperation on our part, at baptism, wherein we receive both the divinely appointed means, and the divinely appointed pledge, that such things may be effected and are effected in us by God.

1) The Christian life takes its starting-point in baptism. It is the condition of entrance into the kingdom of heaven (John 3:5), and by it men are to be made disciples of Christ (Matt.

28:19).

2) In the command of Christ (Matt. 28:19) baptism is made to bear an equally prominent relation to the Father, the Son, and the Holy Spirit, for this very reason, because the Holy Spirit, who by means of baptism begins His work in man, is both of the Father and of the Son (John 14:26; 15:26; 16:7), and that which begins in a man in and by means of baptism, is the gracious presence and activity of God the Holy Ghost and a putting on of Christ (Gal. 3:27), which communion with Christ, may be briefly characterized as a fellowship of death and life with Christ (Rom. 6:4, 5; Col. 2:12; Phil. 3:10).

3) Baptism is the washing of regeneration and renewing of the Holy Ghost (Tit. 3:5) so that our life is hid with Christ in God (Col. 3:3), and the indwelling of the Holy Spirit bears the shape of first-fruits (Rom. 8:23), which is also a guarantee or earnest of future complete redemption of our hearts (2 Cor. 1:22; 5:5; Eph. 1:14).

4) This dawn of light in our heart is compared to the creative fiat of God, who caused the light to shine forth out of darkness (2 Cor. 4:6), and this work of the Holy Spirit can only retain its creative character when all our life in Christ is preceded by a living presence of Christ in us through the Holy Spirit, so that we no longer live to ourselves (Gal. 2:20) but become a life for Him who died and rose again for us (2 Cor. 5:15).

5) In all that takes place in baptism there is not an acting of ours, but an acting and an internal, real, and effectual relation of Christ, of which he becomes a partaker, whom Christ desires to make a sharer of the same according to His will ratified in His word and sacrament. A convert like Paul requires the same, and receives it at his desire (Acts 22:16), just as much and in the same way as it is bestowed upon the little children who

cannot as yet desire it, but who are brought to the Lord by those who know what Christ desires to be and become to the child also, as to everyone who is born of the flesh. That all flesh stands in need of baptism, and that the promise of Christ concerning baptism is valid for all flesh, forms the ground on which rests the certainty of that faith in which infants are brought for baptism, and not a command or law enjoining infant baptism. In John 3:5 stands a plain declaration which applies universally to all, and is a divine ordinance. He, who on God's ordinance and promise brings the child for baptism, acts according to God's will. There exists no greater seal of all subsequent faith than baptism, by which the Lord Jesus Christ owned me, and freely gave me His fellowship even before I was able to desire it. He alone can cradle himself in false security, who desires to attain the blessing of baptism without faith, and forgets the warning words against a wicked, unbelieving heart (Heb. 3:12).

All that is effected and accomplished in us by the divine birth has for its object to form the permanent ground of a growing and conscious life. This becomes obvious to our consciousness in a twofold form, as a joyful resurrection and putting on of the new man through the power of the God who forgives our sins, and a sorrowful dying and putting off of the old man (Rom. 6:3-6; Eph. 4:22-24). For that Christ who desires by the Holy Spirit to take up His abode in us, and to make us like Himself, is no other than He who has passed through death unto life, through suffering unto glory.

1) A change of mind never takes place or continues without a godly abiding sorrow preceding it (2 Cor. 7:10). There is no life with Christ without a dying with Him, no partaking of His dominion without sharing His endurance, no partaking of His

glory without participation in His sufferings (2 Tim. 1:11, 12; Rom. 8:17).

2) The work and working of the Spirit implanted at baptism are to put us in mind of all that Christ has said (John 14:26) and by this word it will be shown whether the spirit within thee is the Spirit of God, who has sealed the word in baptism. And if thou wishest to find thyself in Christ, then hast thou to seek and find thyself not in the incomprehensible spirit of thy regeneration, but in Christ's word. All the phenomena connected with the faithful believer, who is born of God and has arrived at a consciousness thereof, will always be concentrated in the blessed confession: "Lord, to whom shall we go? Thou hast the words of eternal life. And we have believed and know that thou art the Holy One of God" (John 6:68, 69).

II. The Appropriation of the Spirit of Regeneration in our Conversion.

It is the will of God the Creator and Redeemer, that what He bestows upon us by the working of the regenerating Spirit, should be appropriated by the conscious individual, and should be voluntarily embraced by Him. There is so much the more reason for this, in that the working of the regenerating Spirit has for its object to subdue the selfish will, and to awaken in us a life in which we no longer wish to live unto ourselves. Freedom to this end springs from a working of the Spirit of God upon our spiritual nature, by virtue of which God Himself renders it possible for us, in Him and through Him, to be able to will that which is of God.

1) We must ever remember that our life in Christ can in no wise begin without a fundamental and actual relation of God

in Christ to our spirit, which occurs through the work of the Holy Spirit at our baptism, when we put on Christ (Gal. 3:27).

2) This actual relation of God to us becomes a blessing only when it is presented to our consciousness in a series of effects, whose common characteristic is, that we become aware of them as impulses of our own will, the causality of which we are unable to find in ourselves and our own nature, but in God alone. If this new relation, into which God in Christ through the Holy Ghost enters with us, is to become one full of effect in us, and one that shall stimulate our will, this can only be accomplished by the taking place of an actual mutual relation between God and the spiritual basis of our nature.

3) When we divest ourselves of self-will, the will becomes free for the enjoyment of that freedom which is essential freedom, because it is not of ourselves, but of God. This is the sense in which Luther bids us distinguish between self-will and free-will. "We never rightly name or understand free-will, unless it be adorned with the grace of God, without which we should rather term it self-will than free-will".

4) Freedom, according to Scripture, exists only where the Spirit of the Lord is (2 Cor. 3:17). And just when delivered through Christ from his selfish nature, does the man who is so delivered by Christ actually become the servant of Christ (1 Cor. 7:22). And in this relation he experiences what true freedom is. For only when the Son makes us free are we truly free (John 8:36). It is a law of the Spirit of life that makes us free in Christ Jesus from the law of sin and death (Rom. 8:2).

Such willing to do God's will is not the work of man, but of God. The work of God attains the object at which it aims only by a voluntary, self-appropriating, but still self-abjuring action of the individual, and is perfected by an inward deed and an inward acting on the part of man. It is only where that inclination of the heart, never to be separated from God's active working, exists, voluntarily to enter upon that which God causes us spiritually to experience, that the design and end of the regenerating Spirit is attained in the conscious man.

1) The causality of that movement that takes place in the spirit of man, is to be sought not in man, but in God alone. The operation itself is, however, a stirring of the spirit of the Creature by God, a making alive, a quickening.

The operation of God's Holy Spirit precedes all inward acting of the will, and works in us that disposition of the heart which determines our will in conformity with that of God. We are also to regard as the working of God's Spirit, on the one hand our anguish of conscience, and on the other our yearning after peace with God, which inclines us to lay hold of that which God in Christ is for us and has done for us.

1) Christ is the Reconciler of the rupture between God and man. But He is so not as the denier, but as the affirmer of this rupture. He does not so deliver us from the accusations of conscience and the judgment of the law, that He should deny their truth and righteousness; but He affirms both, since He vicariously allows the sentence of the law to take effect in His own person, and perfects the triumph of God's mercy over righteous judgment. Such he desires by the working of the Holy Ghost to make known to our inner experience.

2) In our groaning for complete deliverance, the Holy Spirit intercedes for us with groanings that cannot be uttered, for in the ultimate marriage of God's Spirit with man's spirit the sighing of God's children may just as well be described as an utterance of the Spirit of God (Rom. 8:26), and such groaning forms merely the beginning, but ceases with the full possession

of grace. Here below all our anguish of heart forms the dark but permanent background of the bright peace in Christ (Rom. 8:23; see also 2 Cor. 5:4; Rom. 7:24).

3) Christ stands at the door and knocks whenever the Word of God is preached to the unbeliever. If any one listens to this voice, allows the Spirit to work, opens the door, and Christ enters and sups with him, and he with Christ (Rev. 3:20),—this opening of the door on the part of man may be called his conversion. ·

This twofold passive experience wrought in us by God, our anguish of conscience and yearning after peace with God, is the ground which determines us voluntarily to desire what God in Christ holds out to us in His word. And it is the actual disposition of the human will springing from this, which we call, as well at its beginning as in its permanent existence, man's conversion.

1) Luther also employs the word conversion in the same sense. In his Exposition of Hosea he asks: "What is conversion? Nothing else than obedience to the Gospel, which reproves the world because of sin, righteousness, and judgment".

2) It is the same use of the word which the older dogmaticians designated intransitive conversion as distinguished from transitive conversion, which latter is the fundamental operation of God in us.

3) Our earlier divines distinguished conversion in its narrower sense from regeneration, and indeed attributed the latter to the baptized infant, but not the former. And they were fully justified in so doing. For conversion is not a question of a relation of God to us, which once for all has really taken place, and has at its entrance a complete existence, but is a question of a procedure on man's part, which has its course, its beginning

and its progress, in short its vicissitudes, and can be explained only from the nature of man, and the relation in which he stands to the operation of God who works in us.

4) In regeneration I fix my gaze steadfastly on the great power of God; in conversion, on man's great weakness. Conversion, even if it has once decidedly happened, yet here below moves on only as a continual turning from and turning to, and progress is made with much infirmity.

God is the Cause of Conversion.

The whole history of the doctrine of free-will shows us that there is a consistent position between that which refers the whole work to man and that which attributes all to God.

God is the proper cause of conversion, and therefore the whole cause.

Select Literature

In the following select literature no attempt is made to give a complete bibliography, but only such books are named as are of especial value in the study of the subject. We do not include the Works of the great Lutheran Dogmaticians, nor of the most prominent writers on General Dogmatics of other denominations, as a select list of these is given in my Introduction to Dogmatic Theology. The Literature in German is given very fully in LUTHARDT'S *Kompendium der Dogmatik* and in his *Kompendium der theol. Ethik*.

1. Ante-Nicene Fathers. 10 vols.
2. BECK, Outlines of Biblical Psychology. 1877.
3. CREMER, Biblico-Theologlcal New Testament Greek Lexicon. 1880.
4. DELITZSCH, System of Biblical Psychology. 1869.
5. DORNER, System of Christian Ethics. 1887.
6. FLEMING, Moral Philosophy. 1884.
7. GOESCHEL, Der Mensch nach Leib, Seele und Geist. 1856.
8. HAGENBACH, History of Doctrines. Edited by H. B. Smith. 2 vols. 1862.
9. HARLESS, System of Christian Ethics. 1880.
10. HASTINGS, Dictionary of the Bible. 5 vols.
11. HEARD, The Tripartite Nature of Man. 1885.
12. HODGE, Systematic Theology. 3 vols. 1895.

13. KEERL, Der Mensch das Ebenbild Gottes. 1860.
14. KOESTLIN, Theology of Luther. 2 vols. 1897.
15. KRAUTH, Conservative Reformation and its Theology. 1871.
16. LAIDLAW, The Bible Doctrine of Man. 1883.
17. LUTHARDT, Kompendium der Dogmatik. 1893.
18. LUTHARDT, Fundamental Truths of Christianity. 1869.
19. LUTHARDT, Moral Truths of Christianity. 1873.
20. LUTHARDT, Saving Truths of Christianity. 1868.
21. LUTHARDT, Lehre vom freien Willen. 1863.
22. MUELLER, JULIUS, The Christian Doctrine of Sin. 2 vols. 1868.
23. NAVILLE, Problem of Evil. 1872.
24. Nicene and Post-Nicene Fathers. First Series. 14 vols.
25. Nicene and Post-Nicene Fathers. Second Series. 14 vols.
26. OEHLER, Theology of the Old Testament. 1883.
27. RAND, Classical Moralists. 1909.
28. RAND, Modern Classical Philosophers. 1908.
29. SARTORIUS, Doctrine of Divine Love. 1884.
30. SCHAFF-HERZOG, Encyclopedia of Religious Knowledge. 12 vols.
31. SCHMID, Doctrinal Theology of the Evang. Lutheran Church. 1899.
32. SEEBERG, History of Doctrines. 2 vols. 1905.
33. Standard Bible Dictionary, 1909.
34. STRONG, Systematic Theology. 3 vols. 1907.
35. THAYER, Greek-English New Testament Greek Lexicon. 1894.
36. THOLUCK, Die Lohre von der Suende, etc. 9th edition. 1870.
37. TULLOCH, Christian Doctrine of Sin. 1876.

38. VAN OOSTERZEE, Christian Dogmatics. 2 vols. 1874.
39. WEISS, Biblical Theology of New Testament. 2 vols. 1882.
40. WINDELBAND, History of Philosophy. 1901.
41. ZOECKLER, Die Lehre vom Urstand des Menschen, etc. 1880,

Examination Questions

EXAMINATION QUESTIONS ON ANTHROPOLOGY.

Introduction.

1. As review, how may the subject of Dogmatics be divided?
2. What seven topics will be discussed under Anthropology?
3. Under what four heads will the topic, Man, be treated?

I. MAN.

1. Creation of Man.
    4. How does Hollaz define Man?
    5. What, in general, may we learn from the first two chapters of Genesis?
    6. What does Quenstedt say of the mode of production?
    7. What, in a summary, does Delitzsch say of Gen. 2: 7?
    8. Of what two elements did man originate?
    9. Present Oehler's view of the origin of Man.
    10. Why do we quote Delitzsch and Oehler so fully?
    11. What is the teaching of Pantheism?
    12. What is the favorite hypothesis of our day regarding the

origin of man?

13. What, in substance, does Zoeckler say of the doctrine of Evolution?

14. What can be said of the theory of spontaneous generation?

15. What does the eminent scientist and geologist, Dawson, say of the antiquity of man?

2. The Essential Constituents of Man.

16. In what sense is man trichotomous, and in what sense dichotomous?

17. Show that spirit and matter are essentially opposed to each other.

18. Name three errors which hindered the acceptation of the biblical view.

19. What is the biblical view according to Delitzsch?

20. What is the Old Testament view according to Oehler?

21. What does the Old Testament teach concerning the heart?

22. What, according to Weiss, is the New Testament teaching concerning the nature of man?

23. What is the position of Materialism?

24. How may we answer materialistic opinions?

3. The Unity of the Race.

25. What is the scriptural doctrine concerning Man?

26. Show that history and science confirm Scripture.

27. What proof does Zoeckler present?

28. What does Dr. Krauth say of the importance of this doctrine?

29. What three principal hypotheses are opposed to the Scripture doctrine?

4. The Propagation of the Saul.

30. What three theories have been held concerning the propagation of the soul?

31. What may be said of the theory of Pre-existence?

32. Criticize the theory of Immediate Creationism.

33. Expound more fully the theory of Traducianism or Mediate Creationism.

34. Give Quenstedt's presentation of the Scriptural proof.

35. Give an outline of the history and defense of Traducianism as given by Delitzsch.

II. THE ORIGINAL CONDITION OF MAN.

1. The Scripture Teaching.

36. How will this topic be discussed?

37. Expound the true idea of man.

38. Define more exactly the meaning of the divine image in man.

39. In connection with its psychologic importance, what five facts does Delitzsch emphasize?

40, In what sense does the image of God lie in the Spirit of Man?

41. Define more particularly the triplicity of the human spirit.

42. How does Scripture regard the office of the nous or mind?

43. Illustrate from Scripture the intimate relation between the nous or mind and the logos or word.

44. Define more particularly the Scripture usage of the term spirit of the mind.

45. Explain more fully the three points which we emphasize in the primitive state of man.

ANTHROPOLOGY

2. The Church Doctrine.

46. What was the teaching of the Greek Fathers?

47. Of the Latin Fathers?

48. What was the teaching of Peter Lombard and Bonaventura?

49, What is the teaching of Roman Catholicism?

50. What is the teaching of Luther?

51. What is the teaching of the Apology?

52. Why does Calovius call it a state of integrity, and why of innocence?

53. What does Hollaz say of the meaning of image and likeness?

54. How does Quenstedt define image?

55. What does he say of the perfection of intellect?

56. What does he say of the perfection of will?

57. What does Hollaz say of the purity of the natural affections?

58. Define original righteousness, according to Calovius.

59. Define the three corporeal excellencies.

60. In what did the happiness of the original condition appear?

61. Show that this divine image was not a superadded gift.

62. What is the teaching of Arminianism?

63. Of Socinianism?

64. Of Rationalism?

65. What is the theory of certain speculative theologians?

66. What is the popular scientific theory?

EXAMINATION QUESTIONS

III. THE FALL.

67. Under what topics do we discuss the Fall?
68. Show that the Scripture narrative is historical.
69. In what does the importance and magnitude of the Fall reveal itself?
70. What confirms the Bible narrative?
71. What was the aim of the tree of knowledge?
72. What does Delitzsch say of the Fall?
73. What was the true cause of the Fall?
74. What seven facts may be learned from Gen. 3?
75. Show that the serpent was the tool of Satan.
76. How does Hollaz define the effects of the Fall?
77. How does Delitzsch draw a distinction between the primal sin of Satan and the sin of our first parents?
78. What is the position of Modern Criticism?
79. Of Philosophy?
80. What reasons can be given that the narrative is neither allegorical, mythical, or figurative?

IV. ORIGINAL SIN.

1. Scripture Doctrine.
81. Under what three heads will we discuss original sin?
82. Show that the Old Testament teaches the Universality of Sin.
83. Prove it from the New Testament.
84. Show from Scripture the present character of the unregenerate nature of man.
2. The Church Doctrine,
85. What, in general, was the teaching of the Greek Church?

ANTHROPOLOGY

86. What was the teaching of Justin Martyr?
87. Of Clement of Alexandria?
88. Of Origen?
89. Of Athanasius?
90. Of Gregory of Nazianzus?
91. Of Chrysostom?
92. What, in general, was the teaching of the Western Church?
93. Of Irenaeus?
94. Of Tertullian?
95. Of Cyprian?
96. Of Ambrose?
97. Of Augustine?
98. What, in general, were the views of Pelagius and Celestius?
99. What were the seven propositions of the Pelagians?
100. Criticize Pelagianism.
101. What discordant views prepared the way for Semipelagianism?
102. What were the views of Cassian and Faustus?
103. What was the result of the discussion, and who finally completed the work of Augustine?
104. What were the views of John of Damascus?
105. Of Anselm of Canterbury?
106. Of Peter Lombard?
107. Of Thomas Aquinas?
108. What is the teaching of the Roman Catholic Church?
109. What is the teaching of Lutheran Protestantism as expressed in Art. II. of Augsburg Confession?
110. Give the fourteen points of Krauth's lecture on Original Sin.

111. Show that belief in Original Sin belongs to the very essence of Lutheran faith.

112. Under what seven points does Krauth develop a true doctrine of man?

113. What five facts does Science establish in favour of the Unity of the Race?

114. Define Traducianism, or mediate Creationism.

115. Define the state of integrity.

116. Show that God cannot be the cause of sin.

117. Show that the moral character conditions the state of the will.

118. What four distinct acts did the sin of our first parents embrace?

119. What five lessons can we deduce from the Fall and from the time of the operation of Original Sin?

120. Prove from Scripture that all human beings born in the course of nature are tainted by Original Sin.

121. Prove that Original Sin is transmitted with natural propagation and is hereditary.

122. Prove from Scripture that Original Sin is universal.

123. Show that the effects of Original Sin are both negative and positive.

124. Against whom does the Lutheran Church affirm the doctrine of Original Sin?

125. Under what eight points does Krauth argue that Original Sin is truly sin?

126. Develop the thought that Original Sin has the relations and connections of sin.

127. Prove from Scripture that it has the name and synonyms of sin.

128. Develop the thought that Original Sin has the essence

of sin.

129. That it has the attributes of sin.

130. That it does the acts of sin.

131. Show from Scripture that it incurs the penalties of sin.

132. Prove from Scripture that it needs the remedy of sin, 1) as to its essence, 2) as to its author, and 3) as to its means.

133. Show that Original Sin is conformed to a true definition of sin.

134. Under what nine points does Krauth discuss the great truth that Original Sin condemns and brings now eternal death?

135. Discuss under ten points the momentous truth that Original Sin brings condemnation and eternal death to all who are not born again.

136. What are the last four main points of the discussion?

137. How does the Apology restate the definition of the Augsburg Confession?

138. Under what eight points does it maintain the correct view against false views?

139. What eight points do our Confessors maintain against the Scholastics?

140. Under what six paints do they establish that their definition of Original Sin is not new?

141. Show that their definition agrees with that of Augustine?

142. And with the wiser Scholastics?

143. Discuss the importance of the doctrine.

144. Elaborate Luther's statement, Original Sin remains after baptism.

145. How do our Confessors elaborate the idea that concupiscence is not merely a penalty, but is sin subject to death and

condemnation?

146. How does Luther state the true doctrine of Original Sin in the Smalcald Articles?

147. What false doctrines of the Scholastics does he condemn?

148. What is the matter of controversy, according to the Epitome?

149. Under what three points is the pure doctrine presented?

150. What four reasons are given for making a distinction between our corrupt nature and Original Sin?

151. How do our Confessors enlarge upon the extent of Original Sin?

152. What four Pelagian errors do they reject?

153. What two Synergistic errors?

154. What three Manichaean errors?

155. What five other distinctions are made?

156. Under what four divisions does the Solid Declaration present Original Sin?

157. State the five points under which they discuss the Scriptural doctrine.

158. What errors of the Pelagians are rejected?

159. What errors of the Manichaeans are rejected?

160. By what four arguments do they show that we must distinguish between corrupted human nature and Original Sin?

161. State the argument from the Article of Creation.

162. From the Article of Redemption.

163. From the Article of Sanctification.

164. From the Article of Resurrection.

165. What do our Confessors say of the term "nature"?

166. Explain the statement, Original Sin is not a substance,

but an accident.

167. What distinction do our Dogmaticians draw between Original Sin originating and originated?

168. Why called Original Sin?

169. How do they define Original Sin?

170. What is it called in Scripture?

171. Give the Scriptural proof of the existence of Original Sin.

172. What facts does Chemnitz deduce from Rom. 5:12-14?

173. In what form does Original Sin manifest itself?

174. What are the particular parts of Original Sin?

175. What are its consequences?

176. Although laying stress on natural inheritance, show that our Dogmaticians also teach the imputation of Original Sin.

177. What does Quenstedt say with reference to Rom, 5:12?

178. How does he distinguish between immediate and mediate imputation?

179. What are the adjuncts of Original Sin?

180. What four things must we take account of, in considering Original Sin.

181. Show that Original Sin is not the substance of man.

182. Discuss the topic of the immaculate conception of Virgin Mary.

3. Modern Criticism

183. Trace the development of Unitarianism in the States?

184. What is the tendency of its teaching with reference Original Sin?

185. What is the teaching of Arminianism with reference Original Sin?

186. How does American Methodism differ from Wes-

leyanism?

187. How would you briefly criticize Methodism with reference to their views of Original Sin?

188. What are some of the main points of the Federal theory?

189. Briefly criticize this theory of imputation.

190. What position does Rationalism take?

V. THE ESSENTIAL CHARACTER OF SIN.

1. Scripture Doctrine.

191. Define the origin of sin.

192. Show the successive steps to prove that sin is of free choice.

193. What are the three steps in the process of the origin of sin?

194. What then is the real principle of sin?

195. Show that the real principle of evil does not lie in matter.

196. Show that Gen. 3:22 does not refer to God as an envious Being.

197. What reference to the fall of Adam in the later books?

198. What do you have to say about the Old Testament names for sin?

199. What is the most common name, and its meaning?

200. What is the meaning of 'avon?

201. Of pesha'?

202. How does Delitzsch distinguish between the last three words?

203. What is the meaning of resha'?

204. Of 'aven?

205. What figure underlies many of these terms?

206. What is implied in hamartia?

207. In parabasis?
208. In parakoe?
209. In paraptoma?
210. In agnoema?
211. In hettema?
212. In opheilema?
213. In anomia?
214. In what five different senses is sarx used?
215. On what three constituent elements of sin is emphasis laid?
216. What are the consequences of sin?
217. Thetically stated, name what sin is negatively.
218. What sin is positively.
219. Why is sin not a substance?

2. The Church Doctrine.
220. How is sin defined by our Dogmaticians?
221. What is the cause of sin!
222. Show that God in no sense is the author of sin.
223. Where is the seat of sin?
224. Show that original sin is voluntary.
225. Show that we cannot limit sin to a voluntary transgression of the law.
226. Show that sin lies in the condition of the will.
227. What is the objective aim of sin?
228. What are the consequences of sin?
229. Define *reatus culpae*.
230. Define *reatus poenae*.
231. What is the rationalistic view of sin?
232. In opposition to false views, what is the true view?
233. What is the operation of sin?
234. Criticize the great work of Julius Mueller.

235. What points does he discuss under sin as transgression of law?

236. Under sin as disobedience against God?

237. Under sin as selfishness?

238. Under the imputation of sin?

239. Name the five principal theories of sin he examines.

240. How does he answer those who derive sin from the physical imperfection of man?

241. Those who derive sin from man's sensuous nature?

242. What can be said with reference to Schleiermacher's view of sin?

243. Discuss his theory more fully, and state his main error.

244. State the theory, and give brief historical sketch, of those deriving evil from the contrasts of life.

245. How would you answer this theory?

246. State and answer Hegel's theory of evil.

247. Why can we not accept the dualistic derivation of evil?

248. What testimony does Julius Mueller give as to the importance of the doctrine of sin?

VI. SINS OF ACT.

1. General Definition.

249. Under what two headings is this topic discussed?

250. Illustrate from Scripture the principle underlying actual sin.

251. Show that sin is really a turning away from God.

252. Show that its real root is selfishness.

253. Define actual sin.

254. What names are given to actual sins in Scripture?

2. Divisions of Sins of Act.

255. Define voluntary sin.

256. Define involuntary sin.

257. Define a four-fold sin against conscience.

258. Of what two-fold distinction can we speak of sin in respect to the purpose of the will.

259. Distinguish between a sin of ignorance, of precipitation, and of infirmity.

260. Give Scripture examples of the sin of infirmity.

261. What sharp distinction does Julius Mueller draw between a sin of precipitancy and of infirmity?

262. Define a mortal sin.

263. Define a venial sin.

264. Discuss how this distinction of mortal and venial arises.

265. What can be named as the causes of the forgiveness of venial sins?

266. Name the seven so-called deadly sins.

267. What is the difference of Roman Church and Protestant Church on this topic?

268. What fundamental principle lies at the difference between mortal and venial sins?

269. When may the sin of another be imputed to us?

270. Distinguish between sins of the heart, lip, and deed.

271. Define sins of commission and of omission.

272. Explain Tit. 2:12.

273. What crying sins are referred to in Scripture?

274. What five reasons are given why one sin is more grievous than another?

275. Distinguish between a hidden and open sin.

276. Distinguish between a dead and living sin.

277. Distinguish between an abiding and forgiven sin.

278. Define sin connected with hardness of heart.

279. What is the cause of this hardness?

280. How does Hollaz explain Ex. 7:3.

281. Distinguish between pardonable and unpardonable sins.

282. How did our older Dogmaticians define the sin against the Holy Ghost?

283. In what does its form consist?

284. What adjuncts does Quenstedt name?

285. Why is it not forgiven?

286. What does Julius Mueller say of the moral state necessary?

287. Explain his statement, "It is not only the greatest, it is the most spiritual of sins".

288. Show that its essence is hatred of whatever is known to be divine and godlike.

289. Show that this sin is only another form of "the man of sin".

290. Show that it is connected with the highest revelation of God.

291. Does this sin presuppose regeneration? What are the two views?

292. What does Julius Mueller say?

293. What important truth does this involve?

294. What does it imply subjectively on the part of the person committing this sin?

295. Had the Pharisees committed this sin?

296. Show that the way of return to God is never closed to anyone.

ANTHROPOLOGY

VII. DOCTRINE OF FREE WILL.

1. The Scripture Doctrine.
    297. Show that sin is an abuse of freedom.
    298. Prove from Scripture the moral bondage of sinful man.
    299. Show from Scripture that a relative morality can be attained.
    300. Show that there is no fellowship of man with God apart from grace.
    2. The Church Doctrine.
    301. What was the opinion of Clemens Alexandrinus?
    302. Of Origen?
    303. Of Irenaeus?
    304. Of Gregory of Nazianzum?
    305. Of Chrysostom?
    806. Of Tertullian?
    307. Of Cyprian?
    308. Of Ambrose?
    309. What was the teaching of Pelagius?
    310. What, on the other hand, did Augustine teach?
    311. What was the position of Semipelagianism?
    312. Briefly give a history of the condemnation of the heresies of Semipelagianism and Pelagianism.
    313. What was the tendency of Roman Catholicism?
    314. What was the teaching of Thomas Aquinas?
    315. Duns Scotus?
    316. Gabriel Biel?
    317. What is the teaching of the Roman Catholic Church in the Council of Trent?
    318. What is the teaching of Luther?
    319. Of Melanchthon in his purest period?

EXAMINATION QUESTIONS

320. Summarize the teaching of the Augsburg Confession.
321. Of the Apology.
322. Describe the synergism of Melanchthon.
323. Describe the later synergism.
324. Describe the opposition of Flacius.
325. What is the question at issue, according to Formula of Concord?
326. What does it teach concerning the natural man's knowledge of divine things?
327. Of his will?
328. Of his conversion?
329. Of the causes of conversion?
330. Of the condition of the natural man?
331. In what sense does it teach man is worse than a stone?
332. What do our older divines, in general, teach?
333. How do our Dogmaticians state the question clearly?
334. How do they show that the natural will is free?
335. How do they give a true definition of free will?
336. Show that they teach that the natural man is completely destitute of free will in spiritual things.
337. That he has liberty of choice in regard to what is evil.
338. That be has liberty of choice in external things.
339. How do they illustrate this by the two hemispheres?
340. What was the tendency of the period of transition?
341. Of Sartorius?
342. Of Hase?
343. Of Schleiermacher?
344. Of Julius Mueller?
345. Of Martensen?
346. What position do our modern Lutheran Theologians take?

347. How does Harless describe the working of the Spirit in its beginning?

348. How does he explain the effect of baptism?

349. How does it display its working?

350. When is man truly free?

351. Describe the cause of man's conversion.

352. Show that the Holy Spirit not only begins but completes the work of conversion.

353. Distinguish between transitive and intransitive conversion.

354. Distinguish between regeneration and conversion.

355. What does the history of the doctrine of free will show to us?

356. Name ten of the best works treating of the doctrine of man.

Made in the USA
Coppell, TX
11 May 2025